PRAISE FOR
THE COST OF FEAR
BY MEG STONE

"In this intriguing debut treatise, Stone . . . argues that common advice on how to react when threatened with rape and sexual violence is rooted in sexism. . . . This is sure to stir debate."

—*Publishers Weekly*

"Stone provides a practical, deeply needed resource that expands rather than diminishes the world for women."

—*Booklist*

"*The Cost of Fear* delivers a compelling critique of the shortcomings of conventional safety practices. Through meticulous evidence-based research and personal stories, Stone suggests more effective strategies for eliminating gender-based violence."

—WENDY ROUSE,
author of *Her Own Hero*

"Meg Stone offers her incredible knowledge with love and compassion, an essential guide for resistance-based self-defense training. Drawing from her decades-long experience, Stone empowers you to build mental resilience and vital techniques for developing situational awareness to defuse gender-based violence quickly for your safety. *The Cost of Fear* is a must-read for people of all genders and ages, regardless of their fitness and experience levels."

—REV. IRENE MONROE, co-host of
All Rev'd Up on Boston Public Radio

"Meg Stone has written a powerful, accessible, and devastatingly acute analysis of the pervasiveness of gender-based violence and why our efforts to prevent it have failed, packed with expert insight drawn from her decades-long career and practical tips to empower women and others who are targeted. *The Cost of Fear* moved me, enraged me, and educated me. I don't think I'll ever stop thinking about it. I wish this book weren't necessary. But until we live in a better world, get this book."

—ALEX MARZANO-LESNEVICH,
author of *The Fact of a Body*

"In *The Cost of Fear*, Meg Stone weaves together stories—from the individual to the organizational—and extensive research to offer a comprehensive understanding of the problem of gender-based violence. She makes a clear, compelling case for safety through resistance to both protect individuals and change society. Valuable for everyone from policymakers to individuals wanting to increase their safety, this book can change the world."

—LAUREN R. TAYLOR,
founder-director of Defend Yourself

“DON’T FIGHT BACK”

OTHER BOOKS IN THE MYTHS MADE IN AMERICA SERIES

"THEY JUST NEED TO GET A JOB":
15 Myths on Homelessness,
by Mary Brosnahan (2024)

"YOU JUST NEED TO LOSE WEIGHT":
And 19 Other Myths About Fat People,
by Aubrey Gordon (2023)

"I HAVE NOTHING TO HIDE":
And 20 Other Myths About Surveillance and Privacy,
by Heidi Boghosian (2021)

"PRISONS MAKE US SAFER":
And 20 Other Myths About Mass Incarceration,
by Victoria Law (2021)

"THEY TAKE OUR JOBS!":
And 20 Other Myths About Immigration (EXPANDED EDITION),
by Aviva Chomsky (2018)

"YOU CAN'T FIRE THE BAD ONES!":
And 18 Other Myths About Teachers, Teachers' Unions, and Public Education,
by William Ayers, Crystal Laura, and Rick Ayers (2018)

"YOU'RE IN THE WRONG BATHROOM!":
And 20 Other Myths and Misconceptions About Transgender and Gender Nonconforming People,
by Laura Erickson-Schroth and Laura A. Jacobs (2017)

"ALL THE REAL INDIANS DIED OFF":
And 20 Other Myths About Native Americans,
by Roxanne Dunbar-Ortiz and Dina Gilio-Whitaker (2016)

"GUNS DON'T KILL PEOPLE, PEOPLE KILL PEOPLE":
And Other Myths About Guns and Gun Control,
by Dennis A. Henigan (2016)

"YOU CAN TELL JUST BY LOOKING":
And 20 Other Myths About LGBT Life and People,
by Michael Bronski, Ann Pellegrini, and Michael Amico (2013)

"THEY'RE BANKRUPTING US!":
And 20 Other Myths About Unions,
by Bill Fletcher Jr. (2012)

"DON'T FIGHT BACK"

AND 10 OTHER MYTHS ABOUT CRIME, PERSONAL SAFETY, AND GENDER-BASED VIOLENCE

Meg Stone

BEACON PRESS · BOSTON

MYTHS MADE IN AMERICA

BEACON PRESS
24 Farnsworth Street
Boston, Massachusetts
www.beacon.org

Beacon Press books
are published under the auspices of
the Unitarian Universalist Association of Congregations.

Printed in the United States of America

29 28 27 26 8 7 6 5 4 3 2 1

This book is printed on acid-free paper that meets the uncoated paper ANSI/NISO specifications for permanence as revised in 1992.

Text design and composition by Kim Arney

Library of Congress Cataloging-in-Publication Data is available for this title.
ISBN: 978-0-8070-1624-4;
e-book: 978-0-8070-1625-1;
audiobook: 978-0-8070-2330-3

The authorized representative in the EU for product safety and compliance is Easy Access System Europe 16879218, Mustamäe tee 50, 10621 Tallinn, Estonia: http://beacon.org/eu-contact.

CONTENTS

INTRODUCTION Dumb Women Who Get Attacked and the Men Who Try to Save Them 1

PART 1: HOW ATTACKERS BEHAVE

MYTH 1 "Attackers Can Tell Who Makes a Good Victim by the Way They Walk" 45

MYTH 2 "Don't Fight Back. It Will Make the Attacker Angry and You'll Get Hurt Worse." 63

PART 2: WHAT (OR WHO) TO FEAR

MYTH 3 "I Read in the News There's an Attacker on the Loose, So I Need to Be More Careful Out There" 77

MYTH 4 "Treat Anyone Who Looks Out of Place with Suspicion" 91

MYTH 5 "Crime Is at an All-Time High and Going Up" 105

PART 3: WHAT YOU SHOULD NEVER DO

MYTH 6 "Don't Wear a Ponytail. An Attacker Could Grab It." 125

MYTH 7 "Don't Park Next to a Van (Especially White Vans or Vans with Tinted Windows)" 133

MYTH 8 "Make Sure People Can't See Through Your Windows, Especially When You're Undressed" 145

MYTH 9 "Don't Go Shopping Alone. Otherwise You Could Be a Target of Human Traffickers." 149

PART 4: WHAT YOU SHOULD ALWAYS DO

MYTH 10 "Always Take the Elevator. Attackers Hide Out in Stairwells." 163

MYTH 11 "Always Trust Your Intuition" 169

CONCLUSION How to Be Safe(r) in an Evidence-Poor World 177

Acknowledgments 183

Notes 187

Index 207

INTRODUCTION

DUMB WOMEN WHO GET ATTACKED AND THE MEN WHO TRY TO SAVE THEM

I'm sitting on a folding chair in a room used for group exercise classes. The hardwood floors are unreasonably shiny; no scuff marks betray the constant presence of gym shoes. The walls are a soft, soothing color, maybe yellow. The room is packed. The man at the front is lean and muscular. His Police Academy polo shirt and slacks are unwrinkled; his hair is cropped. His charisma and authoritative tone seem practiced and comfortable.

He's here to give a lecture on personal safety, called something like "Street Smarts for Women." The sponsor is this women's gym, the kind of gym that costs more than $150 a month to join. The kind of gym that has a whirlpool and sauna in a locker room that is never dirty.

About one hundred women sit in the audience, some on the edge of their chairs. Fear and urgency are heavy. It's only been a few weeks since a bright and promising twenty-four-year-old was abducted from an ATM where she'd stopped to get cash after a morning workout—a morning workout at this gym. She was found dead a few hours later, her body dumped in a nature preserve and discovered by a bicyclist.[1] Every woman in this room, I imagine, has stopped at an ATM on her way home from the gym, and maybe they came to this lecture feeling desperate to avoid becoming like her.

The man is affable. Funny even. I don't remember the specifics of his jokes, only that the laughter was loud and cathartic. He tells us what "smart" women do. They don't wear headphones in public. They don't let FedEx or UPS drivers enter their offices, especially if they're the only one still at work. For that matter they don't work late alone. They try to avoid going shopping alone, and if they absolutely can't, they don't buy more than they can easily carry. He does a comedy routine in which he imitates a woman weighed down by too many shopping bags, struggling to balance, eyes on her phone instead of the street. Some people laugh. My arms are folded tight across my body, my jaw is clenched.

Other women, I'm sure, were killed in the two or three weeks it took to plan this lecture. Women whose murders were not covered relentlessly by local news, with remembrances of their favorite songs, or warm personalities. Indigenous women, for example. On some reservations, Native women are murdered at rates ten times the national average. Homicide is the third-leading cause of death for Indigenous women and girls between ten and twenty-four years old, and the fifth-leading for women between twenty-five and thirty-four.[2] Or Black women, who are more than twice as likely to be murdered than white women. A study published by the Violence Policy Center found that 61 percent of Black women murdered in 2018 were killed by intimate partners.[3]

But this young white woman could be us (or at least the "us" that is assembled in a high-end women's gym). All she did was stop at an ATM. And maybe her murder won't scare us so much if we let a confident, charismatic man tell us what to do.

He tells us that if a creepy guy is following us, we should get on our phones. We should pretend we are calling our boyfriends, we should say a man's name loud enough that the creepy guy hears. We should tell our fake boyfriend that we see him in the window, that we are almost home and he should expect us soon. We should tell our fake boyfriend there is soup in the fridge for dinner and that he should start heating it up. It's only been a few minutes since he told us that being on our phones is bad, but still.

I raise my hand and ask the question I always ask at lectures like this one: *What is the evidence that supports the effectiveness of this strategy?*

His answer is not an answer. Something about how he doesn't have time to get into all that and how we should use common sense.

My question is less than sincere. I know what the evidence shows. I've been teaching self-defense for decades, and I know what it means to trust my body, instead of relying on an imminent boyfriend (and a fake one at that) to protect me. I know, too, that sometimes I forget that as a woman I'm supposed to live with a constant, low-grade fear that someone will assault me. I walk alone at night. I wear earbuds in public. I go shopping alone and buy as many groceries as I need. I trust that I could stop an act of violence with my own unremarkable strength. I know, too, that after I took my first feminist self-defense class, I stopped enduring my father's too-tight hugs. I spoke up more in male-dominated spaces. I had always believed that sexism was wrong, but after having the visceral experience of fighting off a male instructor who outweighed me by a hundred pounds, I was more able to embody my beliefs.

Feminists, Black liberation activists, and others committed to social justice have been teaching self-defense for decades.[4] Helping people find their voices and the power of their bodies, helping them become bolder, not more afraid. Helping people make connections between their individual experiences of fear or vulnerability and the political inequities that rely on keeping some people smaller. Yet in the public imagination, self-defense is often understood as an action movie, a gun, or a bunch of directives about how we should clutch our keys or cross the street if we see a homeless person.

This reputation is often well deserved. I've lost hours of my life listening to men tell audiences as white and female and scared as this one what to do: If you're a woman living alone, put a pair of men's boots outside your back door. Don't get undressed in front of a window. Don't wear a ponytail; it's easy for an attacker to grab. Trim your hedges so an attacker can't hide in them. Don't do laundry alone. Pull the fire alarm. Every rapist is afraid of firefighters and apparently will wait for them to show up before they start attacking you. Don't go out alone after dark. Restrict your life to be safe. Depend on the good men to protect you from the bad ones.

As the lecture goes on, I get angry. Angry because I'm just as charmed by the police officer at the front of the room as every other woman seems to be. He's charming in a way that makes me want to like him. And worse, some deep unconscious part of myself wants him to like me.

He gives us a hypothetical situation. We are told to imagine that a guy is creeping us out. The buildup is dramatic. He follows us down the sidewalk. We try to lose him in a crowd but we can't. He leers and makes obscene gestures. When we get to the subway station, he follows us down the stairs. Our intuition tells us to leave the subway station. But we have to get home, or we want to go shopping, so we stay on the subway platform wishing this creepy man would go away.

Your gut instinct is telling you to leave, he tells us. *Every fiber in your being is telling you to leave, you know this guy is up to no good. But if you don't trust your intuition, and you get attacked, whose fault is that?*

"The person who assaulted you," I yell out. Not raising my hand. Not waiting for him to call on me. My arms still tight across my chest.

I can't throw him off for long. He recovers quickly, he's good at public speaking. *Well yeah*, he says, acknowledging and dismissing me at the same time. But he moves right on with his point, which is that women don't trust their intuition and they put themselves in vulnerable situations and then they shouldn't be surprised when they get attacked. I mean what did we expect.

A lot of us feel reassured when someone offers us certainty in the face of a horrible crime against someone who could have been us. Especially someone who didn't do anything to lose the status of "perfect victim"—someone young and white and middle class. With no known history of drug use or sex work, someone whose parents loved her and who are devastated that her bright future was cut short by a brutal stranger.

Every bit of the grief this woman's family experienced deserves respect and empathy and attention. But we can hold that grief or outrage or heartbreak without losing sight of the statistical realities of violence, and we can do so in a way that honors the memory of a beloved person who should still be alive.

The family of Vanessa Marcotte, who was murdered at age twenty-seven by a stranger while she was out walking, is an admirable example of what it means to hold this kind of nuance. Her loved ones started a foundation to honor her memory, and in a video explaining their work, Caroline Tocci, a board member who is Vanessa's cousin, speaks about violence with clarity. "Murder is very rare, but assault isn't," she says.[5] The Vanessa T. Marcotte Foundation gives grants to support mentorship and self-defense training for women and girls, violence prevention education for children and teens of all genders, and domestic violence services. All of these are programs that address the statistical realities of violence.[6] And they run to honor Vanessa's memory because she loved to run. They hold a 5K race every summer and sponsor teams for marathons in a few different cities. They do this instead of telling women not to run or chastising them for running alone.

But too often we are told to diminish ourselves, to avoid "creepy" strangers and trust the police, though some research shows that police officers are more likely than people in other lines of work to be abusive to their spouses.[7] We are told that the people who want to rape or abduct us lurk in poorly lit alleyways. They hide in parking garages, waiting to grab us if we dare to be distracted by our phones or carry too many shopping bags or fail to get a security guard to walk us to our cars. They are outsiders, deviants. Never our friends or loved ones. Never the charming and hilarious person we just met on a date or at a party. Never upstanding members of the communities we call home. When they tell us be "smart," we are to understand that being smart has nothing to do with thinking, reasoning, or analyzing. Being smart about crime is all about complying and following. If you question the advice or the evidence that supports it, you will be met with condescension.

I'm a class-privileged white woman. I was raised on a steady diet of *Law and Order: SVU* to keep me scared and romantic comedies to keep me believing that the power of my love can make men change. If I had a different line of work, I might think twice about grocery shopping after dark, or I might call a friend and stay on the phone with her while I walked to my car in a parking garage. I might have had better things to do with my time than to scour the internet looking for reliable data about crimes in parking lots. (Most of what I found was outdated or taken out of context by companies that sell parking lot security products.)[8]

If I had a different line of work, I might feel afraid in situations in which my chances of being struck by lightning are only a few hundred times less than my chances of being struck by a man in a ski mask who jumps out of the bushes.[9] (A man who is probably Black or Brown in a lot of our imaginations, but we know better than to be explicit about that.)

It's been more than ten years since I sat on that folding chair in that spotless group exercise studio. The girls in the first high school self-defense class I taught through IMPACT Boston, the abuse and violence prevention organization I lead, are hovering around forty now. But the questions I got from the girls I taught last year have changed surprisingly little:

> *If someone approaches you, should you tell them your boyfriend will be right back?*
>
> *I heard you should pretend you don't speak English. Is that right?*
>
> *I heard you should always take the elevator because attackers hide out in stairwells and they will tape your mouth shut so you can't scream, is that real?*
>
> *I heard you shouldn't scream or fight back, that it will just make the attacker more angry.*

On the first day of some of our self-defense classes, we ask students to tell us what they've been taught about how to be safe. If the group is all or mostly girls, the responses come quick, remarkably similar from one group to the next. Don't go out at night; don't talk to strangers; don't accept things from strangers; don't wear revealing clothes; don't be on your phone in public.

I once taught a group of mostly white teenage boys who were quiet and confused when I asked what safety advice they'd gotten from adults or the media. "Wear a seat belt?" one kid finally said. "Be careful crossing the street?" said another. "Don't go to a bad neighborhood," offered a third, but when I asked them what made a neighborhood "bad," nobody wanted to say. More recently, in a racially mixed class, a group of Black boys told us they'd been taught to keep their hands visible and talk softly if they were approached by the police. Others said their sisters and girl cousins got advice that they didn't. When I asked what advice their families gave only to the girls, they told me they didn't know. A boy from a Muslim family came up to me after class to say that his sister had been warned not to wear a hijab in public.

My teaching experience is not systematic like high-quality research, but the gender differences I've observed are consistent with the evidence. Through in-depth interviews with college students on a suburban campus, criminologist Shannon Jacobsen found that a majority of the women—and none of the men—avoided certain places or activities in order to be safe. One participant said she decided not to enroll in a class that met at night. Almost all the women but only a third of the men said they had walked around campus in groups to avoid violence. When the research team asked follow-up questions, they discovered that the men walked in groups to protect their female friends while women said they felt safer walking in groups that included men.[10]

A specific image of crime and how to avoid it lives in a lot of our imaginations. And what some of us fear most is shaped not by the strongest evidence but by the most compelling stories. Management professor Chip Heath and entrepreneur Dan Heath provide insight into what types of ideas stay with people, or "ideas that stick."[11] Chip Heath and his students reviewed hundreds of compelling ideas, presented in formats ranging from proverbs to urban legends to advertising campaigns to often-repeated stories, some of which were true and others were not.

They identified the common characteristics of ideas, beliefs, and stories that stick with us. First, they are simple but also unexpected. They fill voids in our knowledge in ways that are surprising yet uncomplicated. They also have concrete images that are easy for people to picture. In the realm of personal safety advice, that can mean a pair of men's boots on the doorstep of a woman living alone, or telling a woman that if she ever gets abducted and locked in the trunk of a stranger's car, she should kick out the taillight, stick her hand out of the hole, and wave frantically. That way, drivers behind her can see but her abductor can't tell she's trying to get help. Besides, ideas that stick touch our emotions. If people feel something, they're more likely to care. Boring statistics about prevalent problems don't hold our attention the way a single horrifying story does.

A lot of evidence-poor ideas about violence are more compelling than the complicated reality: we have some power to keep ourselves and our communities safer, there are skills we can learn to protect ourselves and our communities, some of those skills have evidence to show they reduce some types of violence, but many more questions can't be answered by quality research. At the same time, structural factors outside our control cause or contribute to violence, and these can be changed only by sustained political organizing. Also, there are some types of safety skills that contribute to creating structural change and others that don't.

Did you fall asleep reading the last paragraph? Did you get lost and have to go back? Did you give up and not care anymore? Most importantly, did you get a compelling picture in your mind as you read it, or are you still thinking about the woman locked in the trunk of a stranger's car who kicks out the taillight and waves her hand at the drivers behind her?

Another characteristic Heath and Heath identified is credibility, having a spokesperson or champion that people believe and trust. In the realm of violence prevention, this one has become the most insidious because the trustworthy spokesperson is often a male police officer. Either that or someone who served in the military or teaches karate or another martial art we've heard of. Most of the research-backed strategies for how to keep ourselves safer come from feminist psychologists, sociologists, and self-defense practitioners, but police departments continue to enjoy a position as leading experts on violence, crime, and safety.[12]

Sexual and domestic violence are widely recognized today because of the work of generations of feminists.[13] As recently as the 1970s, the psychiatric community was convinced that child sexual abuse in families was rare.[14] The first rape crisis centers and domestic violence shelters in the US opened their doors in the mid-1970s. Our current understanding of the magnitude of sexual violence as well as the fact that there are currently 1,300 rape crisis centers and domestic violence service centers in the United States[15] is because feminist activists created service centers, protested police departments, and shaped public opinion.[16]

Still, decades later, it's the police who are seen as the experts. A systematic analysis of the largest national and regional newspapers conducted by Berkeley Media Studies Group in 2014 found that when sexual assault makes the news, law enforcement professionals are more than three times as likely as leaders of rape crisis centers to be quoted.[17] Specifically, 32 percent of people quoted were from the criminal justice system while only 9 percent were leaders of local and national advocacy groups. This study also found that the majority of news stories, 51 percent, were about criminal justice events like arrests, trials, or convictions. Our news media treats law enforcement agencies as experts on sexual and intimate partner violence even though historically, the police were so unwilling to take this violence seriously that they did so only because feminist activists protested police departments and successfully sued them for gender discrimination.[18]

Deciding who to trust when it comes to our safety is complicated. There is something visceral and intimate about when and why we feel vulnerable and the choices we make in an effort to feel less so. Asking hard questions about these beliefs and choices is delicate. Who am I (who is anyone) to tell someone how careful to be? I don't know if the girl asking about pretending not to speak English is a daughter of immigrants who survived harm I will never understand by acting like they couldn't communicate. I don't know if the girl who was told to avoid making an attacker angry heard that advice from her parents. If her parents are kind people who surround her with safe and trustworthy adults, who am I to contradict them with the evidence, especially when the evidence is based on a couple dozen studies that are high quality but don't apply to every possible situation? On the other hand, if her parents are abusive, and they are bombarding her with "stranger danger" messages to undermine her ability to trust her own reality, could informing her that the majority of abuse comes from people we know help her believe she can trust herself? (For my first book, I interviewed a woman who experienced unrelenting sexual and emotional abuse from a martial arts community she thought was her family. The most abusive teacher consistently taught self-defense classes that were full of "stranger danger" messages that directed students to be afraid of people they didn't know.)[19]

Every person is 100 percent entitled to any safety choice that feels right for them, with the exception of choices that stoke racism or prejudice against people with less political and social power. If you have survived a life-altering traumatic experience and the only thing that makes a good night's sleep possible is hiding a knife under your mattress and installing motion sensors on your doors and windows, then you deserve respect for discovering what works for you. If clutching your keys as you walk through a parking lot or keeping your head on a swivel when you're in public gives you peace or relief, then don't let me or anyone else tell you that you're wrong.

And just because an act of violence is statistically uncommon doesn't mean it never happens. So I fully support you in being as vigilant and prepared as you want or need to be. If it feels right to you to avoid dark parking lots, or have a security guard walk you to your car, or carry pepper spray or a whistle on your key chain, I would not presume to tell you to substitute my judgment for your own. You may have a well-thought-out safety strategy based on your unique life. If you are part of a marginalized community that isn't well represented by large-scale research, then your own lived experience is likely more useful than national surveys. In either of those cases, I support you in trusting yourself to know better than me or any other expert what is best for you.

That said, if you are questioning the advice you've been given, I want to offer you the evidence and its limitations. I want to tell you what the research shows and what it doesn't. I want to help you discern what we know from credible sources from what men in authority just say because it sounds good. Maybe they sincerely believe that they are helping, or maybe they think their position entitles them to tell you what to do. I especially want to invite you to think critically about two types of safety directives: those that perpetuate racism and stigma, and those that make you feel like you are wrong, that if you experience violence it's your fault because you parked too close to a white van or wore a miniskirt to a club or used your phone in public.

Here are some common characteristics of baseless safety advice:

- It is given by people who rely on their position of authority as a reason we should listen to them, rather than giving solid evidence or reasoning. If we question the advice or try to determine what evidence supports it, we are dismissed or belittled.
- It casts our mundane decisions or ordinary routines as dangerous. It does so even when there is little or no evidence that any remarkable number of people are assaulted while doing activities like using a public bathroom or climbing a flight of stairs.
- It uses words like "always" or "never" as if every situation is identical and every person's life is the same. It doesn't

account for differences in demographics and life circumstances that are relevant to the ways that people are targeted for violence. Even among women, prevalence of different types of violence varies widely by everything from how old you are to where you work.

- It is irrelevant to the majority of violence, particularly the types of violence and harm that are caused by powerful and privileged people or people we know, love, and are supposed to be able to trust. The most obvious version of this is advice for avoiding sexual violence that can be used only with strangers.

I don't want you to subordinate your critical thinking and good judgment to baseless advice. Nor do I want you to diminish yourself or restrict your life to avoid being attacked. And if you have some privilege, like I do, I really don't want you to confuse your personal safety with perpetuating racism and stigma. One example of this happened in May 2020, the same day Minneapolis police officer Derek Chauvin murdered George Floyd. A white woman named Amy Cooper made a 911 call.[20] She told the operator that there was an African American man threatening her and her dog, and that she didn't feel safe. The man, Christian Cooper, is an avid birdwatcher. They were in an area of Central Park where dogs are required to be leashed to protect the birds and other wildlife. When Christian told Amy to leash her dog, she responded by calling the police. Christian began filming, and the video of Amy making the 911 call went viral on social media. Amy made a second 911 call, falsely claiming that Christian had assaulted her.[21]

I want you to have the fortitude to improve your safety in ways that also upend the power inequities that are so often connected to abuse and violence. I want you to have carefully considered strategies to resist violence, and I want those strategies to be relevant to reality, not stereotypes.

Especially if you are a woman or LGBTQ+ person, I want you to be able to recognize coercive control from people you know, as that is a common precursor to sexual and intimate violence. I want you to have the support to challenge the messages you got that you should be "nice" or that any concern you have is somehow "overreacting." Still, no matter who we are and how much more prevalent some types of violence are than others, none of us have zero chance of being attacked by a stranger who jumps out of the bushes or follows us to our car in a shopping mall, so I also want you to have some skills and principles you can use to decisively protect yourself in the moment if you are attacked. Having useful self-defense skills for an unexpected situation means you don't have to spend as much psychic energy being afraid. (For a deeper dive into specific practical strategies, I recommend *Get Empowered: A Practical Guide to Thrive, Heal, and Embrace Your Confidence in a Sexist World*, by Nadia Telsey and Lauren R. Taylor.)[22]

BUT WHAT IF THEY SAY THEY WANT TO "EMPOWER" YOU?

Fat activist Aubrey Gordon identified some insidious changes to the prevailing public conversations about weight loss. Blatant references to "being on a diet" were socially accepted decades ago, but are much less popular today. "Increasingly, the rhetoric of dieting and weight loss is seen as falling out of favor," she says.[23] "Even one of the most enduring diets in the United States, Weight Watchers, has changed its name to WW, and reoriented its marketing toward more holistic 'wellness' branding." But, she argues, replacing the word "diet" with a different word doesn't make it any less fatphobic: "Weight loss methods are not marketed as diets, but as 'lifestyle changes,' 'detoxes,' 'cleanses,' and 'cognitive behavioral therapy.' That shifting allows the weight-loss industry to cloak its same old diets in the language of holistic wellness and self-care . . . We may talk about diets differently today, but social mandates to become thin are as strong as ever."[24]

A similar repackaging of tired, baseless patriarchal messages exists in the realm of women's safety. Blatant messages telling women to subordinate ourselves to our male protectors may not be socially acceptable outside of "tradwife" and other right-wing spaces,[25] but much like a "cleanse" is just a diet in disguise, a lot of people and organizations that peddle "women's empowerment" are not interested in women having any real power.

Rape Aggression Defense (RAD), the largest police-led self-defense program in the US, has some messages in its manual that communicate respect for the women who take their classes. The "Participant Expectations" section of the manual includes several trauma-informed statements, including "You have every right to choose non-participation at any time for any reason." The page ends with "You are in control of your participation" in big, bold letters. Yet, this message that women have options and agency is side by side with statements about what women should always or never do, framed not as suggestions or options but as directives. These directives include everything from how thick the curtains on our bedroom windows should be to how we should trim our hedges to prevent intruders from hiding in them.

The National Rifle Association (NRA) has a personal safety course called Refuse to Be a Victim. It was initially developed for women in 1993 and, according to the participant manual, went coed in 1997 because of demand from men. The manual opens with an acknowledgment that personal safety is not one size fits all. "Every situation is different, just like every person is different," reads a paragraph from the section on being mentally prepared to avoid crime. "There are no right answers or reactions so you will need to decide for yourself how you will react."[26] The handbook also presents accurate information about child sexual abuse and sexual assault of teens and young adults, stating that most people who abuse are someone the child or teenager knows and trusts.

But after a few empowering messages and a little bit of accurate information, the rest of the manual is devoted to unnuanced directives and unsubstantiated claims about crime and criminals. "Do your laundry with a friend or neighbor," the manual directs, and "Don't do your laundry early in the morning or late at night."[27] There are other directives that are given solely to women. "If you are a woman alone in the house or apartment and a stranger asks to speak to your husband or the man of the house, tell them he is working in the garage or office and cannot be disturbed. Never tell a stranger that you are home alone."[28] "In parking garages, use caution in stairwells. It is usually much safer to walk down the auto ramp instead of using the stairs (provided that you watch out for traffic)."[29] Or, to avoid carjacking, "always allow at least a car's length of space between you and the car in front of you when stopping for traffic signals."[30] Have the authors of this manual ever driven in a city before? I live in Boston, a small congested rude city where people honk at you if you take your foot off the brake pedal a millisecond slower than they would have, then cut you off for any reason or no reason at all. If I left a whole car length in front of me, my nerves would be shot from other drivers' yelling and honking, or I'd never make it anywhere because other drivers would cut in front of me.

A page devoted to women's safety tips from the Louisiana Sheriff's Association opens with an empowering message: "While statistics are extremely high, women need not view themselves as helpless victims."[31] The page includes some reasonable advice about the best ways to use physical skills by focusing on vulnerable targets of an attacker's body: "The eyes, knees, throat and groin are very vulnerable, good places to gouge and kick." The page goes on to acknowledge that the woman in the situation is the best judge of what is best: "But listen to your instincts and try to determine if a counter attack by you is the best approach. If you do decide to fight, make sure your first move is as forceful as possible."

But side by side with these encouraging and reasonable suggestions is the same tired, baseless advice. Always take the elevator, never take the stairs, or if an attacker throws you in his car, "kick out the back tail lights, stick your arm out the hole, and start waving wildly. The driver won't see you, but everyone else will," the directive says. "This trick is said to have saved lives," the Louisiana Sheriff's Association claims, citing no evidence that this has ever saved a life, or even if trunk abductions are prevalent in Louisiana.

Advice like this creates a confusing mess—we can take care of ourselves, as long as we do what men in authority tell us to do. We are not powerless, but we also shouldn't be in the grocery store, the mall, or even the bathroom by ourselves. (Yes, that one is real. It can be found on page 13 of the NRA *Refuse to Be a Victim* manual.)[32]

USING THE EVIDENCE WE HAVE

When it comes to our personal safety, separating fact from fiction presents some specific challenges. We can't base every safety decision on evidence, because gathering the evidence we would need is not always possible. It would be logistically impossible and ethically questionable, for example, to recruit a large group of women and randomly assign them to either clutch their keys while they walk to their cars or not and then measure which group gets attacked more. Also, stopping violence with our own actions is complicated. Most types of violence are systemic and structural, concentrated in communities that have the least political power. So personal safety strategies have to be connected to larger social and political change.

We can't answer every question about every situation, but we can use the evidence we have to evaluate the safety information we are getting. There are three main ways that we can base our personal safety decisions on evidence:

1. Is there actual experimental evidence showing that certain types of strategies or interventions actually reduce violence? (Spoiler alert: the answer to this one is usually no.)
2. Is the safety precaution relevant to types of violence that are actually prevalent? What makes good TV (both fictional drama and the news) is what grabs attention, not what's common.
3. Is this safety precaution perpetuating stigma while deflecting attention from violence perpetrated by people close to us or people in authority who are actually more likely to harm us than random strangers? Does the advice

in question help you recognize and resist coercive control from people you know? Does it equip you with the fortitude to challenge people in authority and make sure leadership is accountable? Most of the widespread sexual abuse crises are in organizations, from the Catholic Church to Olympic Sports to the US military, in which leaders have high levels of authority and it is not safe or even permissible to challenge them.

I deeply believe that structural factors create or exacerbate personal experiences of violence, and the ultimate goal of my activism is to change, upend, dismantle, and reimagine those structural factors. But I also believe that this is a long-term endeavor full of incremental progress and constant backlash. In the face of that reality, people who are targeted for violence have a much more immediate need for practical skills to keep themselves safer. There are ways we can protect ourselves that also contribute to the activism it takes to shift those structural conditions.

SOME QUESTIONS TO HELP YOU EVALUATE A PIECE OF SAFETY ADVICE OR A STATEMENT ABOUT THE NATURE OF VIOLENCE OR CRIME

- Does the advice include a reference to evidence? If you look it up, can you actually find it? (*Don't get me started on the rabbit holes I went down trying to find the statistics about parking lot crime that appear on the websites of companies that sell security products!*)
- Is it relevant to the ways people like you are most likely to be harmed? ("Like you" can mean any number of things: your race, gender, disability status, sexual orientation, age, or how you might be perceived; your job, your housing situation, or the types of activism you engage in.)
- Does it require you to restrict your life? Are the trade-offs of restricting your life clear and do you believe they are worth it?

- Does taking this precaution make you feel more calm or more fearful?
- Does the person giving the advice have an investment in controlling you? (For example, is a familiar person who is harming you teaching you to be afraid of strangers to deflect responsibility from what they are doing?)
- If the statement is verifiably false, who benefits from this particular distortion of reality?
- Who is giving the advice? What is their agenda? (Everyone has one. I make no secret of mine.) Who do they want me to see as someone who could harm you and why? Do you agree with their agenda?

A NOTE ON HOW THIS BOOK IS STRUCTURED

Each chapter starts with a statement about violence, crime, or safety that I believe needs to be debunked. Sometimes the statements are about the nature of violence or crime, and other times the statements are commonly proliferated directives about what people should do to keep themselves safer. I focused on the claims that are most visible in the media (both news and social) as well as the ones that my students ask about the most. In some cases, the statements are verifiably false. In other cases, they are complicated and nuanced. When evidence exists, I present it. When evidence doesn't exist, I suggest some options for how we might evaluate whether this is a precaution we want or need to take.

Each chapter ends with some options for what to do with the information. These options are broken into two sections. "For Yourself" gives examples of what you can do to address your individual, immediate safety (or what the evidence suggests you shouldn't have to worry about). The other section is called "For Social Change," which refers to actions each of us can take to create a safer world or challenge the ways that myths about violence are used to fuel hatred, stigma, and systemic oppression. This goes without saying, but I'm going to say it anyway—if my suggestions resonate with you, take them. If they don't, and you have a thoughtful reason for rejecting them, then the critical thinking you used to disagree with my advice is one of the most important skills you can develop to keep yourself safer!

HOW ARE VIOLENCE AND CRIME MEASURED IN THE US? AND WHO DO THOSE MEASURES EXCLUDE?

Some of the most burning questions we have about violence and safety can be answered by solid evidence, while others cannot.

There has been a consistent underinvestment in developing evidence about violence and safety. Psychologist Randall Waechter found that US government funding for research on sexual violence is between 15 and 81 percent lower than research funding for heart disease, cancer, diabetes, and HIV/AIDS, all of which are less prevalent than sexual assault.[33] And that study was conducted long before the Trump administration tried to squash valuable information about sexual assault, domestic violence, trafficking, and hate violence by branding it as "gender ideology."[34] Our federal government and the philanthropic sector consistently underinvest in violence prevention research, particularly when it comes to types of violence that are concentrated in the least politically powerful communities.

That said, there are some solid and useful sources of federal data about the prevalence of different types of violence and a number of smaller, more targeted studies about what works, what doesn't, and what is stubbornly hard to measure. The largest two data sources about crime or violence in the United States are the National Crime Victimization Survey (NCVS) from the Bureau of Justice Statistics and the Uniform Crime Report (UCR) and National Incident-Based Reporting System (NIBRS) from the FBI. Both of these sources show a consistent downward trend in crime from its height in the 1990s to today.

About the National Crime Victimization Survey

Each year, the United States Census Bureau through the Bureau of Justice Statistics (BJS) conducts a study called the National Crime

Victimization Survey (NCVS). It includes 240,000 people age twelve and older in 150,000 households. The NCVS asks participants if they have experienced nonfatal personal crimes in the past year. Crimes they track are rape or sexual assault, robbery, aggravated and simple assault, and personal larceny and household property crimes including burglary/trespassing, motor vehicle theft, and other types of theft.[35] Survey participants are also asked about their own demographic characteristics, their relationship to the person who victimized them, and the demographic characteristics of the person who victimized them. BJS scientists make efforts to ensure that the people they sample are representative of the US population. Households remain in the NCVS sample for three and a half years and, during that time, are surveyed every six months.

If a person confirms that they have experienced a crime in the last year, researchers ask them a series of questions about the incident. This includes the place the incident occurred (their home, someone else's home, a parking lot, a school). Every incident reported by a survey participant gets its own questionnaire, so if someone reports being victimized multiple times, BJS collects detailed information about each occurrence. NCVS study participants are also asked whether they reported the incident to the police. Most years, around half the NCVS participants say "yes."[36]

This is the advantage of NCVS: given the number of people who don't report to the police, this type of survey research gives a more accurate reflection of the realities of crime. The two major limitations of NCVS are that the prevalence of victimization in the US population of more than 330 million is estimated based on the actual victimization of the 240,000 people who participate in the survey. Also, NCVS relies on self-report, so there is no way to independently verify the incidents.

In addition to questions about whether they reported to the police, the NCVS incident report also includes questions about how people responded to the incident (for example, whether they yelled, physically struck the assailant, or got away) and whether they believe that their self-protective actions made the situation better, worse, or neither.[37] It is our largest and most comprehensive source of evidence about how frequently people resist acts of violence and what happens when they do. Questions to assess self-protection include "Did you do anything with the idea of protecting YOURSELF or your PROPERTY while the incident was going on?" and "Was there anything you did or tried to do about the incident while it was going on?"[38] What follows is a long list of types of self-protection, including fighting back physically, trying to reason with the offender, and trying to get help. Participants are then asked if they sustained an injury, and also if they were injured before or after they took action to protect themselves.

Survey participants are also asked if their self-protective actions helped: "Did (any of) your action(s) help the situation in any way? . . . Did your action(s) help you avoid injury, protect your property, escape from the offender—or were they helpful in some other way?"[39] Survey participants are also asked if their actions made the situation worse. While these data are collected every year and available to the public, not every NCVS result is included in the annual summary reports produced by BJS, and only some findings are the subject of research papers published in peer-reviewed academic journals.

NCVS has been administered every year since 1972. Overall, the survey finds a sharp reduction in crime in the US since its peak in the 1990s. According to one report, violent crime decreased by 79 percent between 1993 and 2021.[40] But some of the most targeted people and communities are not counted in this sharp downward slope: homeless people; people with intellectual disabilities who live in institutions or group homes; youth in the foster care system or youth in state custody who live in group homes; incarcerated people; people experiencing long-term hospitalization for mental health diagnoses; and basically anyone else who is afraid to answer the phone or isn't willing to tell a US government researcher whether anyone has raped, assaulted, or robbed them in the past year.

We don't have research on the scale of the NCVS for the most highly targeted communities, but smaller studies demonstrate that some of the people NCVS excludes may not be experiencing the same decreases in victimization as more privileged people. For example, a study of three hundred women who lived in homeless shelters, single room occupancy (SRO) hotels, or other unstable circumstances found that 87 percent had experienced violence in the past year and 52 percent had experienced two or more types of violence.[41] An analysis of Youth Risk Behavior Survey data from 23 US states found that homeless youth were more than three times as likely to have experienced threats or violence at school in the previous school year compared to those who had stable housing.[42] A study of young adults who had turned eighteen in the foster care system, remaining in state custody without having been adopted or reunited with their families, found that 21 percent were experiencing or perpetrating intimate partner violence, in some cases, both.[43]

Even for people who are included in NCVS, there are cultural and external factors that impact people's safety. Violence linked to social and political inequity is not declining as consistently as other types of crime. Even before the Covid pandemic sparked increases in anti-Asian hate violence, the US Department of Justice found no significant decrease in race-based violence between 2005 and 2019.[44] Also, between 2017 and 2018, the first year of the #MeToo movement, the number of people telling the NCVS they'd been raped almost doubled, from 1.4 victimizations per 1,000 people in 2017 to 2.7 per 1,000 in 2018. The BJS found no statistically significant changes in other crimes between 2017 and 2018.[45] In the 2019 survey, the number had returned to much closer to its previous levels, 1.7 per 1,000 people.[46] The 2019 number proved to be more representative—there were no statistically significant changes in the number of people telling NCVS interviewers they'd experienced rapes between 2019 and 2020.[47] Sociologists Meredith Worthen and Cyrus Schleifer dug deeper into NCVS data during these years and found that the sharp increase in reports of sexual assaults during the height of #MeToo was driven entirely by white women. Though the total number of sexual assaults almost doubled between 2017 and

2018, they found no significant changes in sexual assaults or rapes reported by women of color or men of any race.[48]

In an analysis of federal crime data sources, criminologists Arthur Lurigio and Monte Staton show that the sharp decline in crime we see in year-over-year NCVS data is uneven. Most notably, the declines in crimes seen in NCVS data between 2004 and 2013 were only in stranger-on-stranger violence. They also note that low-income communities of color continue to experience high levels of victimization even while more affluent communities have seen great declines. Also, the relationship between crime and the economy has become less predictable in the last two decades. Violent victimizations, they note, followed economic indicators like poverty, unemployment, and inflation between 1973 and 2000, but that has not been true since 2001. During the financial crisis of 2007 and 2008, the largest economic downturn in 80 years, federal data sources did not show an increase in violent victimizations.[49] Their study was published before Covid numbers were available. NCVS does show an increase in criminal victimization between 2020 and 2021 and again in 2022 but was trending down again in 2023.[50] That said, an analysis of 2023 NCVS data by the Council on Criminal Justice found that while violent victimizations of white people had decreased between 2022 and 2023, violence against Black people had gone up.[51]

Despite its limitations, there are unique benefits to NCVS data when it comes to making choices about our safety. NCVS is the largest and most representative survey of the US population and the largest survey that asks detailed questions about not only crime, violence, and victimization but what people did to protect themselves. That said, other sources may give us better information about the prevalence of sexual and intimate violence. Because NCVS is explicitly about crime, it uses the words "rape" and "sexual assault" that are used in the legal system, so it may not be the most effective measure of this violence. If the person who is harming you is someone you love (or someone you have a complicated relationship with), you may not be willing to use that label. The sharp increase in rapes reported to NCVS in the first year of the #MeToo movement is a perfect illustration of how the public conversation influences the way people understand their lives.

About FBI Crime Data: Uniform Crime Report (UCR) and National Incident-Based Reporting System (NIBRS)

Unlike NCVS, which makes estimates about the US population based on interviews with 240,000 people, the data collected by the FBI represents actual crimes reported to or discovered by the police. Participating city, university and college, county, state, tribal, and federal law enforcement agencies submit their data to the federal government, and then compiled results are made available to the public. Participation is voluntary, police agencies are not required to give their data to the FBI.[52] There are two types of FBI crime data: the National Incident-Based Reporting System (NIBRS), and the Uniform Crime Report (UCR), the latter of which Joe Biden phased out with an executive order in 2021. Before the executive order, police agencies could choose between the more detailed NIBRS or the more general UCR. The main difference between the two reports is that the NIBRS includes more detailed information about crimes. Also, while the UCR captured only the most serious crime that occurred in a single incident (for example, if a person was robbed and stabbed in the same incident, only the stabbing would be counted), the NIBRS captures every crime that is part of the incident.[53] The NIBRS also includes more details of the incident like the relationship between people involved. But as the new system phased in, some police agencies were slow to adopt it. Data reporters Weihua Li and Jasmyne Ricard of the Marshall Project found that in 2020, the year before the transition, almost all police departments in the US submitted data. But in 2021, only two-thirds of departments did so. The numbers improved the following year, but Los Angeles and New York, the two largest police agencies in the US, did not participate.[54]

The advantage of FBI data is that it is based on actual crime reports, not self-reports extrapolated to the population, but there are inaccuracies, some of them deliberate and politically motivated. For example, the City of Atlanta was investigated for purposely underreporting crime to win its bid to host the 1996 Olympic Games.[55] More recently, an investigation by the Marshall Project found that in 2022, Florida governor Ron DeSantis used incomplete data to claim that crime in Florida was at a fifty-year low when in reality the low numbers were the result of missing data. That year, only half of police agencies in Florida reported their crime data, which meant that just over 40 percent of Florida's population was excluded. And while spokespeople for the Florida police claimed that the problem resulted from changes in federal data collection procedures, the Marshall Project's investigation found that Florida had the lowest participation of any US state.[56]

Beyond politically motivated omissions, there are other limitations to understanding violence solely from reports to law enforcement. It reflects the types of crimes that people report to the police or that the police discover, skewing toward communities that trust the police or neighborhoods that have a high police presence. It also skews toward personal crimes like robbery or assault, rather than criminal activity that is embedded in institutions or corporations like wage theft or breaking environmental laws.

Still, the FBI crime data is a valuable source for challenging baseless safety advice. There are countless websites, seminars, and social media videos that tell us to avoid mundane places like stairwells or laundromats. The FBI data can give us perspective on the prevalence of police-identified crimes in these places and help us determine whether we want or need to avoid them. Even though FBI data reflect only those incidents reported to law enforcement agencies that voluntarily participate (or that are located in states that mandate participation), even these trends contradict the advice that so often proliferates. According to the 2023 data, 49 percent of crimes were committed in people's homes. The next most common location is on the street or sidewalk at 20 percent. Also, only 21 percent of crimes included in the National Incident-Based Reporting System were confirmed to have been committed by strangers (28 percent were committed by familiar people, and 28 percent were listed as "relationship unknown").[57]

Other Sources: Public Health Data and the Challenges of Measuring Intimate Abuse and Violence

Some types of violence are stubbornly hard to measure. You can't test someone's blood to determine the presence or absence of sexual assault. Unlike efforts to prevent drunk driving, you can't set up checkpoints to stop people on their way to dates to determine whether they are at risk to sexually coerce. And because the relationships involved in this type of violence are often complicated, it can take years for people to be ready to label the harm they experienced. If a person I don't know punches me in the face, then it's easier and clearer to understand that punch as an assault. I don't have to change anything about my belief system. I don't have to question who I can trust, or have my ideas about safety disrupted. If the person who sexually harms a child is also a trusted mentor who gives the child more time, attention, and encouragement than most other adults, it can be heartbreaking to acknowledge that wrestling and tickling may be part of a pattern that includes overt sexual abuse.

While awareness about sexual violence has changed over time, the changes are often inconsistent. With the spike in reports of sexual assault and rape to NCVS during the first year of the #MeToo movement followed by an almost equal reduction the following year, these changes show us how loaded the words "rape" and "sexual assault" are and how difficult it is for people to connect their experiences to those words.

It wasn't until the 1980s that we had quality evidence that sexual assault was prevalent on college campuses and mostly caused by familiar people. Psychologist Mary Koss is recognized as one of the first researchers to uncover this problem. She is credited with inventing the term "acquaintance rape" at a time when the prevailing belief both inside and outside academia was that most rapes were committed by strangers. After reviewing some ridiculous research proposals from her male colleagues (one of which had women enter a lab wearing bras of different sizes and then asked male study subjects to rate how "rape-able" they were), Koss saw the need to ask students directly about their experiences of sexual violence.[58]

She developed a questionnaire called the Sexual Experiences Survey (SES), which asks about behaviors that met legal definitions of rape or sexual assault but don't use those labels. Some examples of questions from the SES are "Have you had a man attempt sexual intercourse (get on top of you, attempt to insert his penis) when you didn't want to by threatening or using some degree of force (twisting your arm, holding you down, etc.), but intercourse did not occur?"; "Have you had sexual intercourse when you didn't want to because a man used his position of authority (boss, teacher, camp counselor, supervisor) to make you?"; and "Have you given in to sex play (fondling, kissing, or petting, but not intercourse) when you didn't want to because you were overwhelmed by a man's continual arguments and pressure?"[59] Koss has noted the need to make the research more gender-inclusive to reflect the experiences of LGBTQ+ people, but the original research focused on women and initially found that the majority of college women who answered "yes" to one of the behaviorally specific questions also answered "no" when asked directly if they'd experienced sexual assault or rape.[60]

In a commentary published in *Psychology of Women Quarterly* in 2011, Koss notes that while she suspected that more people would answer "yes" to the behaviorally specific questions than questions that used the word "rape," she was not prepared for how great the disparity was. Behaviorally focused language, she found, detected eleven times more incidents than crime-focused language. The first time Koss administered the SES to college students, the final question in the survey was "Have you been raped?" She found that "57% of the women responding affirmatively to the behaviorally specific rape questions denied they had been raped (45% of stranger rape victims and 77% of acquaintance rape victims)."[61] The SES also gives women the opportunity to classify their experience in one of four ways: "I don't feel I was victimized," "I believe I was a victim of serious miscommunication," "I believe I was a victim of a crime other than rape," and "I believe I was a victim of rape."[62] When women were given these options, 92 percent of those whose incidents involved strangers and 89 percent of those whose incidents involved familiars reported that "yes" they felt like they were a victim of something.

Koss also notes that in her earliest surveys, women who answered "yes" to the behaviorally specific questions were compared to those who answered "no" on a large number of attitude and personality measures that were thought to be predictors of victimization. She found, however, that none of these measures of attitude or personality showed any statistically significant differences between the two groups. The only significant difference she found was that "women raped by men they knew were eight times less likely to seek crisis services or report to the police and two times less likely to tell anyone at all."[63]

A lot has changed since the 1980s, most notably the clarity most rape crisis centers in the United States have about communicating the prevalence of sexual violence by familiar people. Still, Koss's research has also demonstrated how stubborn campus sexual violence is. She led a 2015 study that showed that rates of campus sexual assault were higher than they had been in 1985.[64]

The use of behaviorally specific questions to assess the prevalence of intimate violence has become a widespread practice, adopted by researchers in multiple disciplines as well as the United States Centers for Disease Control and Prevention (CDC). Two public health surveys provide useful information on the prevalence of this violence: the National Intimate Partner and Sexual Violence Survey (NISVS), administered to adults; and the Youth Risk Behavior Survey (YRBS), administered to high school and middle school students. (Some of the reports of these surveys have been targeted by Project 2025 and may or may not be accessible through federal websites at the time of publication.)

The first NISVS survey was conducted in 2010, and unlike NCVS, it is not conducted annually. Also, the number of people surveyed is significantly smaller. In an interview that took place before the 2024 election, Kathleen Basile, associate director for science in the CDC's Division of Violence Prevention, told me that the budget for public health surveys is significantly smaller than the resources devoted to studying crime. Like NCVS, population-level estimates are based on the responses of the sample, which is designed to represent the demographics of the United States. Because NISVS is focused on sexual violence, intimate partner violence, and stalking, the survey can be much more thorough in asking not only about intimate violence but also about the impact of this violence on people's health and well-being. NISVS is administered by trained interviewers over the phone. Landlines and cell phones are randomly selected from an autogenerated phone number bank. The most recent NISVS was completed in 2016 and 2017, and included just over 27,000 people.

Similar to Koss, NISVS asks behaviorally based questions rather than questions that name a particular type of crime. Kathleen Basile explained, "If you ask somebody if they were raped, they may not say yes, but if you ask them very behaviorally specific language around their experience, they might say yes." Also, the work of designing questions that can accurately get at the experiences of rape and abuse for thousands of people is difficult. When we spoke, which was before the start of the second Trump administration, the CDC was still evaluating and testing the quality of the questions. Basile explained that they have made so many changes that the surveys are not consistent enough that year-to-year comparisons are meaningful the way they are with NCVS. Additionally, though Koss and her collaborators have created and used successful behavioral measures of sexual assault perpetration in college studies, the CDC stopped asking about perpetration because so few people answered "yes." NISVS is a telephone survey, and it's hard to get people to disclose the harm they've caused to a stranger on the phone. That said, a 2019 research review of studies that included more than 25,000 college men found that 29 percent of them answered "yes" to behaviorally focused questions about whether they had sexually abused.[65]

The most recent data we have available from NISVS show that sexual violence is prevalent in the United States, that it is concentrated in younger people, and that it has impacts on people's health.[66] While more prevalent in women, it affects both women and men (and the survey is not inclusive of gender expansive or nonbinary people). For women, just over one in four (26.8 percent) have experienced rape in their lifetimes, and 2.3 percent experienced rape in the year preceding the survey; 23 percent experienced sexual coercion in their lifetimes, and 3.7 percent experienced sexual coercion in the preceding year. Almost half of women (47.6 percent) experienced unwanted sexual contact other than rape in their lifetimes, and 5.3 percent had this experience in the past year. Additionally, one in three women were sexually harassed in public. More than 80 percent of women who experienced some form of sexual harm were assaulted before they turned 25, and 49 percent were first sexually abused as children. Women with sexual victimization histories reported higher rates of health conditions including asthma, irritable bowel syndrome, headaches, chronic pain, and insomnia. For men, 3.8 percent have experienced rape in their lifetimes, and just over 10 percent of those have been forced to penetrate someone else, and 30 percent have experienced some form of sexual violence in their lifetimes. NISVS also found that 47.3 percent of women and 44.2 percent of men have experienced some form of intimate partner violence.[67] Though serious physical violence and sexual violence by intimate partners were more common for women, the survey recognizes that men also experience significant levels of partner violence. Additionally, NISVS found that nearly one in three women and one in six men have experienced stalking in their lifetimes.[68]

Like NISVS, the Youth Risk Behavior Survey is focused on health. It has been administered in public schools across the US since 1991. Like the NISVS, it originates from the CDC, so the YRBS focuses on behaviors that increase someone's risk of poor health, specifically the changeable behaviors that contribute to the six biggest causes of disease and death in the United States, which include "1) behaviors that contribute to unintentional injuries and violence; 2) sexual behaviors that contribute to human immunodeficiency virus (HIV) infection, other sexually transmitted diseases, and unintended pregnancy; 3) tobacco use; 4) alcohol and other drug use; 5) unhealthy dietary behaviors; and 6) physical inactivity."[69]

Public school classrooms are randomly selected to participate in YRBS. There is some variation from state to state, but the national YRBS survey also asks behaviorally specific questions about sexual assault. Some examples of questions include "During the past 12 months, how many times did *anyone* force you to do sexual things that you did not want to do? (Count such things as kissing, touching, or being physically forced to have sexual intercourse.)" and "During the past 12 months, how many times did *someone you were dating or going out with* force you to do sexual things that you did not want to do? (Count such things as kissing, touching, or being physically forced to have sexual intercourse.)"[70] A 2023 report on findings from all fifty states found that 17 percent of girls and 6 percent of boys reported experiencing sexual violence in the previous year.

That said, young people whose lives make it impossible to regularly attend school are probably experiencing more health risks, same with youth who are incarcerated in juvenile detention facilities that are not included in YRBS. It is also not known how young people who are homeschooled or in private schools that are not required to participate in surveys compare. Also, participation in YRBS requires students to read questions and mark responses on an answer sheet, a process that may not be accessible to some students who are educated in special education classrooms. (Other federal data show that people with intellectual disabilities—the disability most prevalent in segregated public school classrooms—are seven times more likely than nondisabled people to experience sexual abuse.)

While different data sources produce inconsistent information about the prevalence of certain types of violence or crime, it is still valuable to understand. The most useful role the large-scale federal data can play in helping us make choices about our safety is to hold it side by side with the places or situations we've been told to fear or avoid. If our chances of being sexually assaulted in a public bathroom are so low that it doesn't even warrant a fraction of a percentage point in FBI or Department of Justice data, then we can decide that having any particular vigilance about bathrooms may not be the best use of our energy. Also, knowing the facts can help us fight deliberate efforts to instill fear about the safety of public bathrooms as a way to build political will for legislation that prohibits transgender people from using them. As of 2024, thirteen US states have laws that restrict trans people's use of public restrooms, many of which used fear of sexual assault to justify their existence. Yet no lawmaker in any state has ever been able to produce any credible evidence of any transgender person committing a sexual assault in a public bathroom.[71]

Non-Government Data

Sometimes information about violence that comes from journalists and activists is more reliable than what we know from the government. In some cases, violence against socially and politically devalued people is more accurately measured by activists. Other times, the lack of good evidence is because the violence in question is caused by the government.

One example of the latter is data about killings by the police. Beginning in 2014, after then eighteen-year-old Michael Brown was killed by police in Ferguson, Missouri, activists were sounding the alarm about widespread racial profiling and police violence. Journalists at *The Guardian*, as well as other outlets like the *Washington Post*, realized that there was no centralized data about police killings and that law enforcement agencies were not required to report them.[72] To address this, reporters and data scientists created a publicly searchable database called The Counted that included crowdsourced and fact-checked incidents in which police officers shot and killed civilians.[73] In 2015, the first year of the database's existence, *The Guardian* identified more than twice as many police killings as were included in official police departments' reports to the FBI. The availability of this data pressured the FBI to improve its data collection on police violence. The Counted also used data to show that Black people killed by the police were twice as likely as white people killed by police to have been unarmed.[74] Given the brutal targeting of government workers by the Trump administration, the fate of this requirement is unknown.

Other times, people who are highly marginalized are excluded from large-scale crime victimization data even when investigative reporting shows that they experience high rates of violence. This is often the case for people with intellectual disabilities who live in group homes or institutional settings. Large-scale surveys are not made accessible to those who have challenges with communication and comprehension. Yet, investigative journalism has found widespread abuse in these settings. *New York Times* reporters Russ Buettner and Danny Hakim's 2011 investigation revealed a crisis of physical abuse, sexual abuse, and neglect in group homes run by New York State.[75]

Though agencies are required to report serious abuse incidents to law enforcement, Buettner and Hakim found thirteen thousand reports of abuse and neglect, only 5 percent of which were reported. They also uncovered a pattern of incidents in which workers who had physically and sexually abused residents were moved to other group homes rather than fired. Six years later, *New York Times* writer Dan Barry investigated a thirty-year operation in Atalissa, Iowa, in which men with intellectual disabilities were warehoused in barely livable conditions, abused and neglected, and forced to gut birds for a local turkey processing plant for only $65 per week.[76] Despite these and numerous other investigations, it wasn't until the height of the #MeToo movement in 2018 that large-scale federal data on violence against people with intellectual disabilities became public. An NPR series led by Joe Shapiro presented previously unpublished data showing that people with intellectual disabilities were seven times more likely than those without disabilities to experience sexual abuse.[77]

Another example of community-led data collection is the U.S. Trans Survey. Described as "a survey for trans people by trans people," it reaches over ninety-two thousand transgender people across the US with questions about health and well-being, including safety and violence. The 2022 survey found that 30 percent of people had experienced in-person harassment based on gender identity in the previous year and 39 percent were harassed online.[78] The survey also found that 3 percent of respondents were physically assaulted in the previous year and 11 percent were physically assaulted by family members for being trans. These numbers are not captured by NCVS and NISVS, which only reflect violence against men and women and don't give space for people to report being trans.

Indigenous organizers have also collected data to document the problem of missing and murdered Indigenous women and people as well as the severe underreporting of these incidents by government agencies. Organizations like Data for Indigenous Justice, National Indigenous Women's Resource Center, Urban Indian Health Institute, and Sovereign Bodies Institute have launched grassroots data collection and outreach efforts to document the crisis and push the federal government to commit resources to addressing it. Research shows that Indigenous people found dead are more than 135 percent more likely to be unidentified than are people of other races and that most Indigenous women who go missing were last seen in urban areas, despite the stereotype that remote rural areas are the most dangerous.[79] Indigenous-led activist groups have brought attention to the disparities between their grassroots data collection efforts and official numbers. A report by the Urban Indian Health Institute documented 5,712 cases of Indigenous women and girls that went missing or were murdered in 2016, while only 116 were logged by the US Department of Justice.[80]

These disparities underscore that when it comes to crime or violence in the US, many of the most marginalized communities are also the most poorly researched. For people who are part of marginalized communities, the evidence may be irrelevant and safety strategies developed by informed community leaders are likely the most useful.

WHAT THE EVIDENCE SAYS ABOUT PERSONAL SAFETY STRATEGIES

There are few examples of personal safety strategies that have been tested by quality research. A student asks me if they should avoid wearing headphones or pretend they don't speak English, and my response is that there is no good evidence to answer that question. But the one exception to this is the effectiveness of feminist approaches to self-defense for reducing women's risk of experiencing sexual violence. While this research is persistently underfunded or unfunded by US federal agencies—even before the second Trump administration—feminist psychologists, sociologists, and others have consistently found ways to get quality evidence.

In these studies, women who take self-defense and a comparable group of women who don't take self-defense are followed for a year or two, or four. Well-designed surveys that effectively measure sexual assault are given to both groups (usually the Sexual Experiences Survey developed by Mary Koss), and researchers are able to determine that those who got the self-defense class had lower rates of sexual assault victimization than those who did not.

The Enhanced Assess, Acknowledge, Act (EAAA) program, commonly known as Flip the Script, was developed by Charlene Senn for university women in Canada. Flip the Script combines physical self-defense with education that helps women recognize both blatant and subtle sexual coercion. It also helps women define and pursue their own sexual desires. Senn's study of almost one thousand first-year students at three Canadian universities found that women who participated in Flip the Script were 63 percent less likely than a control group to experience sexual assault and 46 percent less likely to experience rape.[81] Senn's study is larger and more sophisticated than most, but its findings are consistent with decades of similar research.

Sociologist Jocelyn Hollander found that women who participated in a self-defense course at a community center in Oregon were 50 percent less likely to experience sexual assault than a control group.[82] Her research on college women found even greater differences between women who took a thirty-hour feminist self-defense course and a comparison group. She found that 9 percent of self-defense students experienced unwanted sexual contact compared to 20 percent of the comparison group, that 4 percent of self-defense students experienced sexual coercion compared to 13 percent of the comparison group, that 3 percent experienced attempted rape compared to 8 percent of the comparison group, and that none experienced rape compared to 3 percent of the comparison group.[83]

Research by Clea Sarnquist of Stanford University found that girls in Nairobi, Kenya, who took self-defense were 63 percent less likely to experience sexual assault. Her research also found that half the girls who participated in the program had used a self-defense skill to stop an attempted assault within a year, and that schools that implemented self-defense programs for girls saw the number of students who dropped out due to pregnancy decrease by almost half.[84]

While researchers caution that the state of the knowledge base is too limited for sweeping conclusions, one article by Charlene Senn, Jocelyn Hollander, and psychologist Christine Gidycz identified the commonalities among the self-defense programs that were shown by research to reduce sexual violence: They explicitly challenge victim blame and place responsibility for sexual assault on those who perpetrate. They encourage women to trust themselves and to look critically at the ways societal sexism affects their intimate relationships. This includes challenging sexist expectations that they avoid conflict by subordinating their wants and needs to men's. Effective self-defense programs focus on sexual assault by familiar people and teach physical resistance skills designed for the realities of gender-based violence. Most of them also include sex education, because when women know what they want out of sexual relationships, it's easier to spot when they're being coerced into doing something they don't.[85]

There is no published research showing that any nonfeminist approach to self-defense reduces any type of violence. There are some published studies of Rape Aggression Defense (RAD), the largest police-led self-defense program in the United States. Founded in 1989 by retired marine and police officer Lawrence Nadeau, RAD has over eleven thousand teachers, most of them college and municipal police officers. RAD programs have been criticized by domestic violence prevention advocates for reinforcing myths about stranger danger and not supporting choice and consent for participants.[86] The program's leadership does make efforts to be trauma informed, but the student manual is full of directives about personal safety that can't be supported by evidence.

The evidence about RAD is decidedly lacking compared to the evidence about feminist self-defense. There are some published studies showing that women had positive experiences of taking the class[87] or increases in self-confidence[88] but also lower levels of confidence in their ability to navigate challenges in interpersonal relationships.[89] No other personal safety program led by police, nonfeminist martial artists, or former military service members has any published research evaluating their effectiveness to stop violence.

Effective educational programs are nuanced. They draw connections between individual agency and societal inequities. They emphasize choice and give people concrete skills to challenge their own subordination. They are a stark and important contrast to most of the safety advice that is available on the internet.

WHEN MEN'S TRAUMA BECOMES WOMEN'S MARCHING ORDERS

In the introduction to his book, *The New Superpower for Women*, retired police officer and self-defense teacher Steve Kardian shares a brave and vulnerable story from his childhood.[90] He was in eighth grade. A football injury put him in the hospital for weeks with a broken back. He was an athletic kid, so being stuck in a hospital bed made him restless. A Catholic priest visited him. Kardian was bored, so he agreed to let the priest into his room.

At first, they talked about school and sports. The priest then asked if Kardian wanted to make a confession. "Figuring it would be a nice gesture—after all he had come to visit at make the time go by faster—I said yes," he tells us.[91] He confessed a few mundane sins like cursing at his brother and talking back to his mom. The priest responded by asking if he masturbated. Kardian remembers being shocked. He remembers lying to the priest, saying he didn't know what masturbation was. In response, the priest pulled down Kardian's underwear and began stroking his genitals. *As a way to explain masturbation*, the priest told him.

As soon as he could, Steve Kardian told his parents what the priest had done. The next thing he remembers is a doctor, the police, and his parents crowded around his bed.

"A doctor stood, taking notes," he tells us.

"One of the cops asked, 'Hey, is he on any medication?'"

His eyes met the doctor's and I saw an understanding pass between them."

The doctor then asked Kardian if the abuse could have been a dream.

His parents never spoke to him about the abuse again. As far as he knows, the priest was not held accountable.

"That brief encounter," he tells us, "taught me what it's like to be on the receiving end of unwanted attention."[92]

Kardian's experience of both surviving abuse and then seeing his experience erased by the institutional power of the Catholic Church, the police, and the hospital fills me with a familiar rage. His parents' inability or unwillingness to face the priest's betrayal is, for me, the heart of the problem. I want to understand why Kardian's parents couldn't or didn't push back and advocate for their son. More importantly, I want to understand what needs to change so that more parents have what they need to protect their kids and hold powerful institutions accountable.

Instead of this experience fueling a commitment to holding the Church accountable or even preventing sexual abuse against people of all genders—particularly the thousands of boys who are sexually abused by Catholic priests—Kardian instead chose to focus his career on protecting women. "During my career in law enforcement, I concentrated on crimes against women," he tells us. "My passion is educating and teaching women about the power of common sense."[93] Fourteen-year-old Steve Kardian did not lack common sense. He was betrayed by the priest and unsupported by the adults whose job it was to protect him.

Watching Steve Kardian distance himself from his own survivorship fills me with a toxic mix of heartbreak, compassion, and anger. Just a few pages before telling us about the abusive priest, Steve

Kardian explained women's unique vulnerability. "While all of us need to take precautions to stay safe," he tells us, "the truth is that crimes against women, along with their psychological, emotional and physical effects differ from crimes against men. The playing field may look the same, but it is a different game with different rules. When a predator attacks a man, the man's money or life, or both, are at stake. When a woman is attacked, her money or life, or both, are at stake, but there is also the real possibility for sexual assault."[94] It's true that adult women experience far more sexual violence than adult men, but according to the CDC and other sources, men and boys do also experience sexual violence.[95] I'm as angry as I am heartbroken when I think about the gargantuan leap he makes from surviving sexual abuse as a boy to the statement that violence against women is caused—or at least exacerbated—by our lack of common sense or our failure to trust our intuition.

In his book *The Power of Awareness*, former military operative and author Dan Schilling is less explicit about exclusively focusing his safety advice on women, and to be fair, a respectable number of the examples he gives of people making poor safety decisions are of men.[96] But his anecdotes about women who make bad decisions are abundant and familiar. There's the woman who was almost raped because she let a strange man into her apartment complex, and the woman who was robbed in an unfamiliar city because her jewelry made her look like a tourist. There's the American woman who chose not to wear a headscarf while walking around an open-air market in a Muslim country, and the teenage girl at the mall who fell victim to a serial killer because he was posing as a police officer and she believed him.

Yet, mixed in with these stories about other people are Schilling's own stories about PTSD. "Losing friends, experiencing and inflicting violence, failing to save someone's life. All of these alter and damage you," he tells his readers in the introduction to *The Power of Awareness*. "I've struggled with all of these things and in some ways always will."[97] Schilling goes on to explain that his safety and risk calculation are a constant part of him. Because of the trauma he's survived, he sees risk and potential for violence everywhere he goes.[98]

I cannot imagine the terrifying violence Schilling or Kardian have witnessed in their work, but I struggle just as much with how it impacts the advice they give. *Be on alert at all times*, they tell their readers, *and if you're not and something happens to you, well what did you expect?* I try to imagine what it's like to do the types of work these men have done. To be called when someone is afraid, and to be expected to risk your own physical safety to save them. I wonder how scared you must feel, and how quickly that fear hardens into anger when the expectations of your job (and maybe your gender) prohibit you from shutting your office door and crying. Especially when you're in a profession that looks down on getting therapy. An anonymous survey of close to eight thousand sworn police officers who are members of the Fraternal Order of Police found that 90 percent believed there was stigma associated with law enforcement officers seeking mental health services, even after critical and traumatic incidents on the job. Of those who believed there was a stigma, 84.7 percent said that they would be concerned about being seen as weak or unfit, and 76.1 percent said that they were concerned that seeking mental health care could put their job at risk.[99]

I wonder if men who survived abuse in childhood and went on to be police officers who respond to domestic violence calls ever get to talk about how it feels to revisit abuse in an adult body, one that is strong and imposing, with a belt full of weapons and the power and responsibility to make people pay for the kind of violence that shaped their young lives. But given the data on mental health stigma, I imagine a lot of them don't.

I struggle with what I see as a mix of unresolved trauma and entitlement that lives in the thick, muscular bodies of men like Kardian and Schilling. I can't imagine the violence they've witnessed. I've had my own experience of dangerous professions—working nights in a domestic violence shelter, or accompanying survivors to court hearings. There were times when ex-husbands approached me in court, or even in the parking lot. There were times I hung up on threatening phone calls, but I was never in the kind of immediate danger that some police officers and military troops are. And I could always shut my door and cry without anybody thinking I wasn't qualified to do my job.

What Schilling is describing in himself is understood in the mental health field as hypervigilance, a common symptom of post-traumatic stress disorder. Psychiatrist Nicole Smith describes hypervigilance as "a state of heightened awareness and watchfulness that has been characterized in survivors of trauma and violence. Hypervigilance is defined as the feeling of being constantly on guard for the purpose of detecting potential danger, even when the risk of danger is low. For people exposed to threat of danger, hypervigilance can fulfill a survival function and increase preparedness. However, excessive hypervigilance, especially for a wide range of danger cues, can be maladaptive. For example, hypervigilance has been associated with a number of negative cognitive and behavioral consequences, including attentional bias, memory impairment, and difficulty with emotional regulation. It also serves to maintain anxiety disorders and post-traumatic stress disorder (PTSD), with anxiety increasing hypervigilance for threat, which leads to greater threat detection and thus more future anxiety and hypervigilance."[100]

In my years of working with survivors and teaching self-defense, I've heard a lot of victim-blaming evidence-poor safety advice from men who I see as hypervigilant. Men who go into self-defense as a way to feel safer and wind up wanting everyone around them to live as they do. Many have not been given the space and support they deserve—that we all deserve—to heal from trauma. This is especially true for those in occupations where the expectation is that they run toward danger to protect the rest of us.

And while Kardian and Schilling put it in books, countless others put it on websites or TikTok or say it in personal safety seminars for women. *I'm going to command you to be afraid of everyday life like I am because then I can see my hypervigilance as a way of being smarter than you, rather than a trauma symptom I have to heal. And if I direct my safety advice at women, then I can be your protector.* "Do you really need to be vigilant when you park the car at the local library or your doctor's office or the gym, when there are plenty of people coming and going?" Steve Kardian asks his readers. "The answer to these questions is yes."[101]

The need for control over one's environment is a recognized reaction to surviving trauma. The problem comes when taking these steps for yourself morphs into imposing them on others. The line between the kind of control that keeps intolerable feelings at bay and the kind that is designed to coerce and diminish other people is not as clear as it needs to be. Too often, safety advice becomes another form of coercive control.

✦ ✦ ✦

I want you to live a bigger and bolder life and, if it aligns with your values, to connect your personal safety to social and political change that will create safety for all. I don't want you to sit through a lecture like the one I endured, being told you're not smart, and that if you persist in being dumb or careless, then you're to blame if someone attacks you. I don't want you to be dismissed like I was when I ask an obvious question: *What is the evidence that supports the advice you just gave me?* I want you to have the information you need to make safety decisions that empower you without harming others, and I want you to develop the skills and courage to challenge people in authority when they try to dismiss or control you. Because the skill and practice of speaking up and resisting when someone is trying to coerce us is the core of preventing violence and abuse. Saying "no" or "I'm not OK with this" or "stop" or "wait a minute" will disrupt the silences and power imbalances in which abuse and violence thrive. Critical thinking, not following simplistic directives, is the real way to be smart.

PART I

HOW ATTACKERS BEHAVE

MYTH 1

"ATTACKERS CAN TELL WHO MAKES A GOOD VICTIM BY THE WAY THEY WALK"

The year I started teaching self-defense, a colleague told me about a study that supposedly explained how attackers choose their victims. He explained that videotapes of people walking down a crowded sidewalk in New York City were shown to men who were in prison for violent crimes. Those men were then asked which of the pedestrians they would attack, and they all chose the same people.

The story was compelling. Neat and satisfying like the formulaic crime dramas I secretly loved. It was comforting and revelatory to think that some large number of criminals would all agree on which pedestrians would be the easiest to attack. It made violence feel controllable. More than that, it gave me confidence that I could avoid it myself and guide my students to walk in ways that deterred crime.

We were careless with numbers back then. Without fact-checking, we repeated statistics we'd heard until they took on a life that had nothing to do with the original research. Ninety percent of communication is body language, we said, or was it eighty? It changed a lot. But our tone was authoritative, and our motives were, for the most part, sincere. We used numbers and studies, I think, to legitimize ourselves. A lot of the people who took our classes were nervous about learning self-defense, and maybe the certainty in our voices made them feel less afraid.

More than twenty years passed between the first time I heard about that study and the day I looked it up. When I did, I realized how overstated my colleague's claims had been. The study, called "Attracting Assault: Victims' Nonverbal Cues," was conducted by psychologist Morris Stein and communications professor Betty Grayson and published in the *Journal of Communication* in 1981.[1] It was a two-part study. In the first part, they asked twelve men who were in prison for assaults against strangers to watch video footage of people walking along a sidewalk in New York City. The incarcerated men saw videos of sixty walkers whom the researchers had divided into four groups: young men, old men, young women, and old women.

These twelve men made judgments about how easy it would be to rob or assault each pedestrian, using descriptions that ranged from "A very easy rip-off" to "Would avoid it. Too big a situation. Too heavy."[2] Grayson and Stein then created a ten-point scale using the men's own words, with one being the easiest to attack and ten the most difficult. They then asked fifty-three other incarcerated men to use that scale to rate the walkers. Of the men in the study, 87 percent were Black at a time when, according to the Department of Justice, only 41 percent of the US prison population was Black.

The fifty-three men were not uniform in how they rated the pedestrians. The number of men who agreed on any given pedestrian was at most thirty-six. With some pedestrians it was as low as twenty-seven, or just over half the sample. Also, some of the characteristics the men identified were not changeable. Older women were overrepresented in the "victim" group, and older men got the highest average "victim" score.

Grayson and Stein spent little time acknowledging the weak consensus or the reality that a lot of people are perceived as vulnerable based on characteristics they couldn't change. Instead, they enlisted two people trained in Laban analysis, a method of classifying and interpreting people's movements, to systematically describe the way the so-called victims had moved. Some research has shown that Laban analysis is imprecise. In a controlled experiment that involved video tapes of trained dancers executing identical movements, a team of certified Laban analysts were not consistent in how they classified the movements.[3]

The analysts who were part of Grayson and Stein's study identified twenty-one categories of movement, only five of which had statistically significant differences between "victims" and "non-victims." Yet even when statistical tests found significant differences, the movements of the pedestrians in the two groups were not wholly distinct. One example is the length of people's stride. Those rated as "non-victims" all had a medium stride, meaning that the steps they took were neither too short nor too long for their height. But just over half the group classified as "victims" also had medium strides.

Other movement differences included how people shifted their weight, how they picked up their feet, and which arm they swung forward when they took a step. Those deemed "non-victims" swung the arm on the opposite side of their bodies as the leg taking the step but so did almost half the "victims" (nine out of twenty).

Despite its limited and questionably meaningful conclusions, this study continues to prop up overstated claims about how attackers choose their victims. A TikTok video by lifestyle and self-help author Michael X, which has several thousand likes, asserts that "when violent criminals in a high security prison were shown video of pedestrians and they were asked who they would pick out to attack, they all chose the same people." They didn't all choose the same people. Still, Michael X claims, "A few seconds of the person walking was all they needed to see."[4] In his book *The New Superpower for Women*, Steve Kardian offers a similar exaggerated claim: "There was a consensus about who would be easy to overpower and control. Every inmate chose exactly the same person," he claims despite the study's much less conclusive results.[5]

The Grayson and Stein study inspired decades of research that attempted to classify potential victims by the way they walk, one of which was published in 2013 and led by Canadian psychologist Angela Book.[6] In an interview, she told me that she became interested in this line of research after reading a biography of serial killer Ted

Bundy.[7] In it, Bundy had asserted that he could tell a victim by how she tilted her head and the way she walked. As a researcher, Book's reaction to Ted Bundy's statement was "Why not test it?" When she describes the conclusions of her research, she tells me she found that "there was a sort of prototypical victim walk."

But if you dive deep into her 2013 study, a more complicated picture emerges. It included forty-seven men incarcerated in a high security Canadian prison for violent crimes. Book, whose expertise is in psychopathy, wanted to determine whether those with more Factor 1 psychopathic traits (like lacking empathy and remorse) would be more adept at identifying people with past history of victimization by the way they walked. The forty-seven incarcerated men watched video clips of twelve college students, eight women and four men, walking from one room to another. Participants were not aware that they were being recorded, which enabled researchers to capture their natural movements, but they later consented to having the videos used in research. After being videotaped, the students answered a questionnaire about whether they had past experiences of abuse or bullying.

Book's team hypothesized that people with histories of violence and abuse walked in ways that telegraphed vulnerability and that people with psychopathic traits would be more attuned to these vulnerabilities. Book's team asked the incarcerated men to rate the walkers on a ten-point scale of how easy or difficult they would be to rob and assault. They then asked the men to give reasons for their ratings.

Like the Grayson and Stein study, the men were not uniform in who they said they would choose to victimize. Also, the strongest areas of consensus were based on traits that were difficult or impossible to change. Of the forty-seven men, thirty-eight identified physical fitness and perceived ability to fight back as a reason to avoid attacking certain people. Thirty-four identified body type, assuming that heavier people would be easier to assault because they would move slower, and thirty-three chose women, who were seen as being more vulnerable than men. Study participants also chose characteristics of the environment, like whether the person was alone or whether the lighting was dim (a combined total of thirty-six people identified one or the other of these). The way someone walked scored lower than all of these traits. Consistent with the research hypothesis, men who met the criteria for Factor 1 psychopathy were more likely to focus on the way people walked.

Like the Grayson and Stein study, these conclusions were based on a small number of incarcerated men viewing an even smaller number of walkers. Also, Book's study had a low response rate—only 50 percent of the men her team approached agreed to participate—and the article doesn't give any information about whether there were meaningful differences between participants and nonparticipants. Still, the existence of a so-called victim walk was the main focus of the researchers' conclusions.

The videos used in Book's prison research were created for an earlier study of college students she worked on, which was led by her colleague Sarah Wheeler.[8] In that study, forty-seven college men who had not been convicted of any crimes were given psychological tests to assess their psychopathic traits. They were then asked to rate the videotaped walkers by how easy they would be to commit "assault with the intent to rob" them. The authors indicate that they asked the men for reasons why they believed certain students were easier to attack, but the research article doesn't include the reasons they gave. Two independent coders rated the students' body movements according to the "victim" characteristics identified by Grayson and Stein.

It's important to acknowledge that the "victim" traits were more prevalent in the six students with past histories of abuse. But while the men who scored higher on the psychopathy scale were more likely to rate the abuse survivors as being vulnerable, they were less likely than study participants with lower psychopathy scores to give the person's walk as the reason for their selection. Unlike Book's prison study, this one doesn't give us information about the other factors that influenced the college men's decisions, so it's hard to assess the difference between changeable and unchangeable characteristics. It's possible that men with higher levels of psychopathy noticed the way people walked but were not consciously aware of why they perceived certain people as weaker than others. It's also possible that they were aware of reading people as vulnerable by how they walked but were not truthful with the research team. Still, despite these unclear findings—and a discussion at the end of the research paper that acknowledges how inconsistent similar studies have been—Wheeler and her team make a bold assertion. "Overall," they contend, "the results clearly support the results that psychopathic traits enable victim selection."

It's well established that people with past histories of abuse and trauma experience higher rates of subsequent violence.[9] But the reasons why this is the case are anything but straightforward. Reducing this complicated reality to the way people move their feet or swing their arms does a disservice not only to survivors but to healers and researchers who are trying to help people shift the patterns of thought and behavior that undermine their safety and well-being. We now have compelling evidence that traumatic experiences ranging from military combat to child sexual abuse to surviving an earthquake or car crash have lasting effects on our brains and bodies. Experiencing trauma can undermine our ability to distinguish dangerous situations from safe ones. Other research has shown that people with PTSD and other conditions related to trauma are more likely than others to freeze when they feel fear. This trauma response, which is natural and human and not anyone's fault, could be exploited by people who want to cause harm.

In the 1980s, psychologist Christine Gidycz was part of the research team that worked on Mary Koss's landmark study, which first established not only how prevalent sexual assault was on college campuses but that the majority of college women who experienced sexual violence were assaulted or raped by someone they knew. In a commentary published in *Psychology of Women Quarterly* twenty-five years later, Gidycz described the gut punch of reading through the questionnaires the women completed.[10] A graduate student at the time, she was responsible for analyzing the data, which involved reading questionnaires college women had completed. In addition to the surprisingly high prevalence of sexual violence, she found that women who had been abused as children or teens experienced more sexual assaults in college than women with no such histories.

Her subsequent research added to the growing evidence base that established past abuse history as a risk factor for future assaults: "we found that women with a history of sexual victimization in either childhood or adolescence were almost twice as likely as women without a history of victimization to be assaulted during a brief (9-week) academic quarter."[11] When she followed women for longer periods of time, she found even starker differences. Those women who were assaulted or raped during the nine-week academic quarter were three times more likely to be assaulted during the next three months of the study. And "those women victimized between the 3 and 6 month follow-up assessments were fully 20 times more likely to be victimized during the 9-month follow-up period compared to women who were not victimized during these time periods."

These findings motivated Gidycz to devote much of her research career to understanding the relationship between unresolved trauma and future experiences of sexual violence. In her 2011 commentary, she described her struggle to find a theory that explained this outcome. She conducted a follow-up study in the 1990s in which she attempted to establish a relationship between victimization and other risk factors like multiple sexual partners or interpersonal problems. She found no statistically significant relationships between these risk factors and victimization, no easy explanation. Other researchers have looked at everything from emotional dysregulation to using alcohol to cope with trauma. Some theories are more possible to substantiate than others, but the problem is more complicated than any one explanation.

The idea of abuse survivors "telegraphing vulnerability" is complicated. It deserves depth and nuance rather than being reduced to a "prototypical victim walk." In her compelling essay collection *Nervous*, author and activist Jen Soriano explores the complexity of how her body holds on to the traumatic experiences she survived.

She understands her chronic pain and related health conditions as a result of personal and generational trauma. She also understands how unique and complicated each survivor's body language can be. "Implicit flashbacks expressed through the body lend themselves more to interpretive theory than factual translation," she says. "The ways our bodies speak are as infinitely varied as each of our life experiences."[12]

Author and former sex worker Lily Burana fiercely rejects easy categorizations of the peep show work she did in Times Square in her late teens and early twenties. "The debate over whether or not sex work is exploitative shrank to a frivolous academic exercise when our bills piled up," she says in her essay titled "Elegy for Times Square."[13] "We were doing what we could with who we were." A survivor of childhood abuse with undiagnosed disabilities that left her unable to thrive in school, Burana describes this risky line of work as her best available option. She is also unwilling to pretend away how traumatizing it was to have to push past her body's limits in order to earn a living. "We coped the best we knew how, and what I couldn't handle has bubbled up, decades later. Just because money makes you say Yes doesn't mean the body doesn't store No in its memory—as sorrow, as trauma." These authors and numerous others explore complex relationships between their histories, their decisions, and the way they experience their bodies. The relationship between past trauma and future abuse is tangled and nuanced. It deserves better than reductive statements about how attackers choose their victims.

Christine Gidycz came to a similar conclusion through her decades of research. She went on to lead studies that identified risk factors for perpetration as well as designing educational programs that help survivors develop the skills to communicate assertively and become more attuned to indications that someone they know is trying to harm them. For some women who grew up in abusive households, coercive control was just normal life. That, coupled with everyday sexism, can make it hard to break free from the socialization that causes our bodies to appear tentative or unconfident.

Even as she documented the extent to which past abuse predicted future abuse, Gidycz remained clear about who is responsible for the problem. Quoting psychologist Liz Grauerholz, she asserts that risk factors seen in survivors do not exist in a vacuum: "Future research needs to consider what distinguishes perpetrators from other men who interact with prior victims and do not take advantage of their vulnerability."[14] Some of her mentees have applied similar research methods to studying perpetration on college campuses and found similar results: college men with a history of sexual aggression were almost nine times more likely than those with no such history to sexually abuse within a three-month follow-up period.

The people Wheeler and Book videotaped were college students. If the abuse and violence they experienced followed predictable patterns, they likely experienced it in their homes, dating relationships, or schools. And at the time the researchers recorded them, they were likely away from that unsafe situation for the first time, meaning they'd only had a few months or years to make sense of the trauma and its impact on their emerging adult lives. Maybe they reflexively kept their heads down or tried to take up as little space as possible because that kept them safer when they were children. Maybe they lacked awareness of their bodies because they'd been numb for most of their lives, their bodies choosing numbness so they wouldn't feel the pain of the rapes or assaults or bullying they'd endured.

Since the publication of the Grayson and Stein study in 1981, researchers have found creative ways to research the relationship between walk and vulnerability. Their methods and conclusions range from interesting to ridiculous. One of the most meaningful studies was conducted in the 1990s by psychologist Jennifer Murzynski.[15] Unlike Grayson and Stein, who recorded people in real-world settings, she and her team videotaped three models with similar features and dressed in similar clothing. Each model walked around the same corner of the same campus building at the same time of day. And each model did three different walks that were choreographed by the research team—one in which they exhibited the traits Grayson and Stein had associated with "non-victims" and the other two walks had two different combinations of "victim" characteristics.

Then, forty-one undergraduates and thirty-three police officers were asked to rate the walkers by how confident they appeared. "Suppose that this woman is on her way to a party where the only person she knows is the hostess," the research subjects were asked. "Imagine that as she walks along she is thinking about the party. How do you think she feels?" The scale ranged from "very confident" to "very unconfident." They were then asked to rate how vulnerable they believed the woman was to sexual assault by a stranger. Specifically, they were asked to "Imagine this same woman is being watched by a would-be assailant. How would you rate her vulnerability to sexual assault?"

By keeping the walker's age, gender, and appearance consistent, and by removing environmental factors like poor lighting, Murzynski's team showed that different ways of walking left research subjects with different impressions. Both the police officers and the students rated the women exhibiting the "victim" traits as significantly less confident and significantly more vulnerable. Of course, more relevant research questions on a college campus would be focused on sexual violence by a familiar person rather than a stranger. But this study demonstrated that the nonverbal communication identified by incarcerated men in the early 1980s also communicated vulnerability to students and police officers more than a decade later.

Other researchers have gone to bizarre lengths to create conditions that isolate a person's walk from their physical appearance or the environment. Some used a technique called point-light analysis, which involved dressing women walkers in black spandex bodysuits, putting black hoods over their heads and then putting pieces of reflective tape on their shoulders, elbows, wrists, hips, knees, and ankles. Walkers were then videotaped in the dark so the research subjects tasked with assessing how vulnerable they looked could see only their joints. The results of these studies, and their relevance to real life, are mixed.

In the early 2000s, psychologists Rebecca Gunns and Lucy Johnston[16] conducted a series of point-light studies on a New Zealand college campus. Women walkers were dressed in these black bodysuits and glow tape and were videotaped as they walked across the floor of a studio in the dark. They were rated by thirty college students (half men and half women). Each walker was recorded in two different scenarios: one in which they were told to walk normally and another in which they were told to imagine they were walking through an inner-city park late at night. The walkers who imagined themselves in the park looked less vulnerable to the study subjects. Their walks exhibited the characteristics Grayson and Stein had identified in the "non-victims."

Gunns and Johnson's team conducted a series of follow-up studies. They found that women who had chosen to take a self-defense course before enrolling in the study appeared less vulnerable than those who had not. Yet, when they randomly assigned study participants to either take a self-defense course or not, they did not notice differences. In a final experiment, the women who had the highest "vulnerability" scores were instructed how to walk according to the Grayson and Stein criteria, and as a result they were rated by students to appear less vulnerable. It's telling that actual self-defense instruction made the walkers appear more confident as did being coached in the Grayson and Stein walking style, but a self-defense course led by the research team did not have the same effect. Again, with a small number of observers who were only able to see fluorescent tape on the location of the walkers' joints, it's hard to know what useful information this study produced.

A series of studies of Japanese university students led by Kikue Sakaguchi[17] compared the point-light technique to a real-world setting. In the first experiment, women walked across a studio with similar dark bodysuits and reflective tape. Afterward, they were asked about three common experiences of unchosen attention from strangers that are prevalent in Japan: unwanted sexual advances, groping of sexual body parts on public transportation, and nonsexual, usually non-traumatizing types of unchosen attention like being asked for directions. The women were then rated by forty-five male students. Those who had short strides and walked slowly were deemed by the men to be more likely to experience unwanted sexual advances and physical groping. Women with short strides were more likely to have rated themselves as being neurotic, introverted, and shy. Sakaguchi's team found, however, that while there was a relationship between walking style and self-reported psychological struggles, there was no relationship between women's walking style and their actual experiences of victimization.

Using an artificial setup is an understandable strategy. It lets researchers separate the way someone walks from their demographic characteristics and the natural environment, so the people rating them can focus solely on their body language. But none of us can be separated from our age or gender or race or disability. No act of abuse or violence can be separated from its context.

Another study conducted by Sakaguchi's team illustrates this point. When the same college women were observed in their real clothing in an environment that wasn't a lab, the women's appearance got more attention than the way they walked. In the second study, women were filmed while walking in a busy subway station wearing the clothes they normally wore. Similar to the first design, they were observed by fifty-three male students. Women who wore high heels and skirts or had an appearance that the men considered fashionable were judged to be more likely to experience unwanted sexual attention and groping. When asked about their own experiences, women who had more traditionally feminine appearances did report higher levels of unwanted sexual attention. But unlike the point-light study in the lab, the women who reported less confidence and more neuroses were not rated as being more likely to experience unwanted sexual attention. When real-world conditions were removed, the Grayson and Stein "victim walk" traits were seen as the primary determinant of vulnerability, but when women were observed in the real world, the way they walked was less influential than their appearance. Also, the men correctly perceived which women received unwanted attention in the subway station, but not in the lab.

In my interview with Angela Book, I asked if she was aware of any large-scale studies of victim selection and walk. She said she was not, and my hours of research didn't produce any either. Book was part of the research team that worked on the most recent and largest walk study. Conducted in 2017 and led by Lindsay Fulham,[18] this two-part study assessed whether hypervigilance, or heightened awareness of surroundings and potential danger, made women survivors less likely to exhibit the Grayson and Stein victim cues. In the first study, 60 college women were recorded walking from one classroom to another without their knowledge, and another 60 women were told they were going to be recorded. All 120 were surveyed about their experiences of sexual and physical victimization. They found that women with abuse histories who were unaware of being recorded were more likely to exhibit the Grayson and Stein vulnerability cues in their walks, while there was no significant difference between survivors and non-survivors who were aware of being recorded. Though the first study claimed to be about hypervigilance, which is usually understood as a PTSD symptom characterized by experiencing innocuous situations as dangerous, they actually measured only awareness.

In a second study, sixty-two participants' walks were each recorded twice—once when they were unaware and again when they were aware. In this study, they were given a questionnaire to measure their hypervigilance in addition to their experiences of sexual and nonsexual violence. Again, they found that aware walkers were less likely to exhibit the vulnerability cues than the same walkers recorded when they were unaware. They also found less change between the aware and unaware conditions in the participants reporting higher levels of hypervigilance. Sexual assault survivors reported higher levels of hypervigilance than those who experienced nonsexual violence or no violence.

With this result and other research, I want to be clear that I don't dismiss the importance of nonverbal communication. But its meaning has to be interpreted with nuance. People who speak the same language can be relatively confident that they share an understanding of the meaning of words like "car," "dog," or "coat." But psychologists who study nonverbal communication caution us against assuming a universally understood vocabulary of gestures, facial expressions, or body positions. Even with the words I gave as examples, when I say "dog," I could be imagining a pit bull while you picture a black lab. And the car in my imagination is a Toyota hatchback with a few too many dents from being parked on the streets in a city known for aggressive drivers. I doubt you pictured exactly the same thing when you read the word "car."

One of the oldest and most constantly misinterpreted studies of nonverbal communication was led by Albert Mehrabian and published in the *Journal of Personality and Social Psychology* in 1967. What the actual study shows is that when verbal communication is inconsistent with nonverbal communication (like frowning and crossing your arms while saying "I'm happy to see you"), then observers are more likely to believe the nonverbal message than the words. When study subjects saw someone exhibit body language that was contradictory to the words they spoke, they found that only 7 percent made a judgment about the speaker's intention by the words, while the remaining 93 percent made their judgments by tone of voice or physical appearance. Over the years, those findings have been misinterpreted to mean that 93 percent of all communication is body language.[19]

That said, some more recent research does show that people make assumptions about others by their gestures, facial expressions, or how they hold their bodies. In a recent study of 1,500 people from three nationalities, research subjects found political speech performed by trained actors to be more persuasive and trustworthy when the speakers' hands mirrored the words they said. They also judged the speakers to be more confident when their feet were shoulder distance apart.[20] A meta-analysis of nonverbal communication on job interviews showed that making eye contact, nodding one's head, and dressing in a way that appeared professional had positive impacts on how people were rated by prospective employers. In some studies, these types of nonverbal communication were more influential in determining whether people got jobs than the substance of their answers to interview questions.[21]

A 2019 overview of the state of research on nonverbal communication led by psychologist Judith Hall and published in *Annual Review of Psychology* reveals some important limitations of the field.[22] Specifically focusing on what psychologists call "interpersonal accuracy," or the ability of one person to interpret the nonverbal communication of another, she notes that studies are correlational, meaning that while a relationship between two variables might achieve statistical significance, psychologists don't have a consensus on a causal mechanism that explains why certain gestures or body positions are associated with certain meanings.

In other words, none of the studies have identified the cause of why perception of another person's nonverbal communication is or is not accurate. In some studies, Hall notes, all the research subjects have to do is perform better than chance to reach statistical significance, so even a significant result is not necessarily meaningful in the real world. Like the walking research, many other nonverbal communication studies have small samples. And exploring the predictive value, or likelihood that study participants guess the answer that supports the hypothesis, is not done consistently.

We can learn useful lessons if we put these findings in perspective—to draw the modest conclusions that the studies deserve rather than the sweeping generalizations that show up in baseless safety advice. Maybe it's comforting to make violence, particularly stranger violence, that predictable: who gets attacked and who doesn't is as simple as how confident you look when you walk. More than that, looking confident is as simple as how you swing your arms or how big your stride is. It's more true—if less satisfying—to say that people who want to harm other people are looking for a number of conditions, some of which we can change and some we can't.

Of course there's nothing wrong with projecting confidence when we walk. Being aware and alert can affect our lives positively (though it's probably more likely to keep you from tripping over a curb or crashing into another pedestrian than it is to help you avoid being selected by a stranger who is looking for someone to assault). But believing that "predators" are monolithic and there is an easy way to avoid being chosen by them does a number of disservices. The most obvious is that it perpetuates victim blame.

It also does a disservice to anyone who is looking for individual safety strategies. Safety advice that defines our risk in simplistic ways diverts us from the skills that make us safer, most importantly discernment and critical thinking. Developing this kind of discernment can help us reflect on our snap judgments to determine whether our reaction to a given situation is racial prejudice, a trauma response, or attunement to a truly dangerous situation. Another is paying attention to when we say "yes" when we want to say "no," and reflecting on why we made that choice. Were we afraid to assert ourselves because of lessons we learned from our culture, our families, or our experiences of abuse? Is our financial survival so precarious that we feel the need to please everyone around us? Are the ways we survived an abusive family or partner no longer helping us? Or are they helping us be more attuned to people we meet who may try to harm us? If we've experienced abuse or violence, it's important to be compassionate and pragmatic in assessing our decisions. Blaming ourselves and feeling bad about our decisions won't help most of us thrive. Cultivating self-awareness, compassion, critical thinking, and useful skills will.

ACTION STEPS

For Yourself

- If you are struggling with past trauma, find a skilled, knowledgeable therapist who can help you heal. For most people, it's best to have a therapist who can create a space that doesn't blame you for other people's decisions to harm you, and who also helps you develop the skills and insights you need to improve your quality of life. This can mean helping you develop new skills to respond to unwanted attention and feel safe enough to clearly assert your needs, wants, and limits. For some survivors this can mean taking risks of your choosing, like having a lot of sex so you can do it on your terms or doing intense sports you once feared. If this is the case, a therapist that helps you make sense of your actions will probably serve you better than one with inflexible ideas of "healthy" and "unhealthy."

- If you are a trauma survivor who freezes in the face of stress, it may be especially helpful to learn some skills to help you break the freeze response. The research of neuroscientist Amy Arnsten and others has shown that the human brain is not built to make complex decisions under stress, so in stressful situations we default to our habits.[23] If you grew up in an unsafe home or were harmed by someone you were supposed to be able to trust, it's probably true that your habits (like freezing, or showing vulnerability, or complying with someone else's wishes) kept you safer. Be kind and understanding toward yourself. Some survivors have found martial arts and boxing helpful, as they provide a safe and controlled environment to experience the power of your body.
- Understand that there is some truth to nonverbal communication, and that using your body to reinforce the statements you make is helpful. Be aware of your gestures, eye contact, and tone of voice as they may help you convey confidence. That said, don't feel compelled to waste energy obsessing about the length of your stride, the way you pick up your feet, or how your arms swing. If it helps you avoid unwanted attention (not just the attention of people who are trying to harm you, but also pushy salespeople or people on the bus who want to suck you into boring conversations), find a style of assertive verbal and nonverbal communication that feels genuine and sustainable.

For Social Change

- If you hear someone tell you that an attacker can tell a good victim by the way they walk, respond by giving them more information about the Grayson and Stein study and the others that it spawned: the sample was small, it didn't represent the demographics of the general population, and the majority of movement categories did not show significant differences.

MYTH 2

"DON'T FIGHT BACK. IT WILL MAKE THE ATTACKER ANGRY AND YOU'LL GET HURT WORSE."

I've lost count of the number of times I've been asked if fighting back will make an assault worse. It's a question I get from adults and teenagers, from private school students and people who live in homeless shelters. From engineers and chemists and accountants who are part of affinity groups for women in male-dominated fields. From organizers and activists, from survivors of abuse and violence.

Even across worlds of difference in class, race, age, and life experience, it always strikes me that so many people, most of them women, have internalized an almost identical message. *Fighting back is dangerous, or it's impossible.* It will make the attacker angrier, some have been told, as if managing the anger of someone who is trying to hurt us is possible or even important.

If I fight, they want to know, *won't I just get hurt worse?*

That message sounds like the threats abusive partners make. Using intimidation to immobilize us, immobilizing us to make it easier for them to overpower us.

That said, not fighting, not struggling, is the best option for a lot of survivors. Especially if they were children, especially if the person hurting them was someone they depended on for housing or food or even love. Sometimes our bodies don't give us the choice, like if we involuntarily freeze in response to a threat.

At the same time, it's just as important to challenge the perception that if someone tries to hurt us, we have no say in the matter.

People who harm other people are not invulnerable. Fighting back (or "victim resistance" as the criminologists call it) can and does work, and most of the available research shows it works more often than it doesn't. The evidence is not as robust or current as I wish it was, but there are no large published studies that found that resistance makes assaults worse. (To be fair, in one smaller study that was based on self-reports of men incarcerated for sexual abuse, 58.7 percent said they reacted violently to victim resistance compared to 41.3 percent who said they reacted nonviolently.)[1]

A lot of our earliest understanding of resistance comes from feminist sociologists Pauline Bart and Patricia O'Brien, who, in the late 1970s and early '80s, conducted an exploratory study, looking for commonalities among women who stopped sexual violence with their own bodies and voices as well as how they differed from those who experienced rape. Through in-depth interviews that addressed everything from birth order to beliefs about gender, they found similarities among women who resisted, some of which are consistent with the findings of subsequent larger studies.[2]

Women who stopped rape with resistance, Bart and O'Brien found, were more likely to have played contact sports as children (Title IX was enacted in 1972), were more likely to have been socialized as children to be outspoken or assertive, and less likely to have been punished for being aggressive. In the moment of the assault, women who physically fought back or yelled and screamed were most likely to stop an assault in progress.

Around the same time, psychologist Sarah Ullman explored this question from the other perspective. She conducted research in a treatment facility for men who had been convicted of sex crimes and sentenced to live there.[3] With her collaborator Raymond Knight, she analyzed police reports, court transcripts, victim impact statements, and other records, which gave her detailed information about the assaults and what stopped them. The men were almost all white—96 percent—and were incarcerated in this facility because they were deemed dangerous to the public. The study included 274 incidents in which these men had attempted to sexually assault women and teens sixteen and older. Not surprising for an incarcerated sample in the 1980s, 83 percent of the incidents involved strangers.

Ullman and Knight found that women who resisted forcefully, by either yelling or physically fighting back, were the least likely to experience rape. Forceful physical resistance and forceful verbal resistance were associated with less severe sexual assaults or no sexual assaults. Nonforceful physical resistance was not related to any increase or decrease in sexual assault, while nonforceful verbal resistance was associated with more assaults and more severe assaults. This study also found that the majority of women, 88 percent, did not engage in forceful physical resistance.

Another important finding is that in situations in which women were injured, they were injured before they resisted, not after. Analysis of resistance that includes time sequences is key—especially to address the belief that fighting back makes an assailant "more angry" and an angry assailant will hurt you worse. Compared to most researchers studying large samples of nonincarcerated people, Ullman and Knight had access to more documentation, including court transcripts of testimony that survivors gave under oath. Because of this, they could put together a more complete timeline of events. When they analyzed the timelines, they found that "the men inflicted the same level of physical injury no matter how the woman responded. The offender's aggression, and *not* the victim's resistance, was responsible for physical injury."

In an interview, Sarah Ullman tells me that having access to so much information about each event helped her establish that injuries women experienced preceded their resistance. "The sequential analysis was able to show this is not just correlation," she told me.

From this study and other early research, Sarah Ullman was among the first to classify resistance into four categories: forceful physical resistance (like hitting, kicking, punching), forceful verbal resistance (yelling), nonforceful physical resistance (pulling away, running, removing someone's hands), and nonforceful verbal resistance (crying, pleading, reasoning).[4]

Later research used larger, more representative samples, often the NCVS. A 2018 meta-analysis by Jennifer Wong and Samantha Balemba illustrates both the consistency of findings and how much more research is needed.[5] Wong and Balemba searched twenty-five academic databases plus technical reports and dissertations and found seven studies of sexual assault resistance. In all cases, they found that resistance was effective. Women who used both physical and verbal resistance were less likely to experience completed rape. Wong and Balemba note that there is inconsistent evidence about whether people who resisted experienced more injuries. But several researchers have demonstrated that when the sequence of events is carefully analyzed, the results show that women who fight back are not more likely to sustain injuries *after* they defend themselves.

One study that was part of this meta-analysis was conducted by Jongyeon Tark and Gary Kleck, including a deep dive into the question of time sequence of injury and assault.[6] Their analysis of ten years of NCVS data found that resisting sexual assaults drastically reduced the number of completed rape: 19 percent of rapes were completed after some form of resistance, compared with 88 percent that were completed when the person did not resist. The NCVS asks people who have experienced an incident to answer detailed questions about it. Tark and Kleck thoroughly analyzed those reports and found that women who resisted did not sustain injuries after fighting back. Their research also found that multiple types of resistance were effective at reducing rape—forceful physical self-defense, yelling, and running away. The only strategy not associated with reduced rates of rape was arguing, reasoning, pleading, or cooperating.

A 2010 study by criminologists Rob Guerette and Shannon Santana analyzed NCVS data from the early 1990s to the mid-2000s and found similar results, that resistance was effective at stopping both robberies and rapes.[7] The people who reported robbery attempts to NCVS were evenly divided between women and men, and different types of resistance reduced the odds of completed robberies by different amounts: verbal resistance decreased the odds by 58 percent and physical resistance by 76 percent, and weapon use reduced it to almost zero (86 percent for knives and 92 percent for guns). They found that white men, however, were significantly more likely than women or people of color of any gender to resist robbery. They also found that the only demographic group who was more likely to sustain injury after they resisted was people of color. By contrast, almost all rape incidents reported to NCVS were from women. Guerette and Santana found that verbal resistance reduced the odds of experiencing rape by 66 percent, physical resistance by 85 percent, and use of a weapon by 91 percent. They also found that resistance was more effective when the perpetrator was a stranger. They did not find evidence of higher rates of injury after resisting.

Criminologist Bonnie Fisher led the largest published study that wasn't based on NCVS data.[8] Her team surveyed almost 4,500 college women who attended 233 different institutions. Participating universities were randomly selected and represented a range of locations (urban, rural, or suburban) and size (measured by total student enrollment). Women who attended these schools were surveyed about their experiences of resisting different types of unwanted sexual attention. Because the survey was more focused, Fisher's team was able to ask multiple questions about the incidents, and the results provide a more nuanced understanding of women's experiences of verbal sexual coercion and physical sexual violence. For each type of incident, women were asked, "Did you do anything with the idea of protecting yourself or stopping the behavior while the incident was going on?"[9] Women who responded "yes" were asked to describe their actions.

They found that 77 percent of women who experienced incidents used some form of protective action and that all women who did something to protect themselves reduced their chances of experiencing a completed sexual assault or rape. The most effective protective actions were those that matched the type of harm—in other words, countering a physical assault with physical resistance or responding to verbal coercion with verbal resistance.

They found that women who used a forceful physical skill were 32 percent less likely than women who used no resistance strategy to experience rape, and those who used a nonforceful physical action were 24 percent less likely to experience rape. Those who used both forceful and nonforceful physical skills were 59 percent less likely to experience rape. For other types of sexual assault, they found that women who used nonforceful verbal resistance were 26 percent less likely to experience assault, and those who used forceful verbal resistance were 21 percent less likely to experience an assault. Women using both forceful and nonforceful verbal strategies were 44 percent less likely to experience this type of assault. The only increase Fisher's team found was women who used physical resistance in response to sexual assaults other than rape, and that increase was 14 percent. In response to sexual coercion, women who used nonforceful verbal resistance were 19 percent less likely to be coerced than those who used no resistance.

This study illustrates the nuance needed to interpret findings about the effectiveness of self-protection. Overall, self-protection reduced the odds of experiencing sexual harm, but the one case in which it didn't deserves further understanding. The reality is, we haven't invested the resources to thoroughly explore questions like this one. Also, no large-scale victim resistance studies have been published in the last decade. When I asked Sarah Ullman why she thinks this is the case, she said it was difficult to get funding to study victim resistance. She had to shift her research focus to other areas because she was not able to get grants to study the effectiveness of self-defense, and that was before the Trump administration cut research funding and threatened to remove important public health data from federal agency websites.

That said, more recent research found that resistance was effective in stopping sexual assaults by acquaintances and dating partners. A 2021 study led by psychologist Lindsay Orchowski surveyed college students about heterosexual sexual encounters that men initiated and women didn't want.[10] Her aim was to determine how often these encounters were stopped and what stopped them. Her team surveyed 635 men and 650 women in their first year of college, asking them about unwanted experiences of sexual touching, intercourse, giving a woman alcohol to facilitate sexual activity, and taking a woman to an isolated location. Women and men differed in their estimates of how many sexual advances were unwanted, how often unwanted sexual activity stopped, and what actions stopped it. But both groups reported that the reason most of the encounters stopped was women's resistance, which Orchowski defined as saying "Stop!" or "No," having a conversation about sexual limits, or using a physical self-defense skill. According to the women, 85 percent of unwanted advances were stopped by women's resistance. The men reported that 73 percent of the encounters were interrupted by women's resistance.

Orchowski's team found some differences in students' reports of how often different types of advances were stopped. Women reported that 85.7 percent of unwanted kissing, 61.9 percent of unwanted intercourse, 80 percent of moving the sexual interaction beyond their limits, 76.6 percent of attempts to give them alcohol they didn't want, and 89 percent of attempts to take them to an isolated location were stopped by women's resistance. Men's reports were not identical, but similar. The majority said that they stopped all types of sexual activity when women resisted.

Resistance to sexual assault is better researched than resistance to other types of violence, but one 2014 study led by criminologist Rachael Powers analyzed nonsexual assaults reported to the NCVS from the 1990s to the mid-2000s.[11] Her team found some notable differences in race, age, and other assault characteristics in terms of people's reports of when and whether they fought back. People were more likely to use forceful physical resistance if they were attacked by someone who had attacked them before. Women were more likely to use forceful verbal strategies while men more likely used forceful physical strategies. Verbal strategies were also more common when the incident happened in a private location (like a home) or when the offender was drinking. This study also found that forceful physical strategies were more common if the offender was known. Unlike the other studies, Powers didn't address the impact of the resistance, so it's not possible from this study to assess what types of victim resistance are most effective for nonsexual assaults.

Usually missing from studies of resistance are the most marginalized communities. One exception to this is a 2012 study of incarcerated women's experiences of resisting intimate partner violence. Criminologists Ráchael Powers and Sally Simpson conducted in-depth interviews with 199 women who were incarcerated in Baltimore prisons.[12] Study participants were asked about their experiences of intimate partner violence in the three years before they were incarcerated. Because most of the women had extensive histories of both surviving and causing violence, they reported a total of 487 incidents. Powers and Simpson found that 80 percent of the incidents involved some form of resistance. Forceful physical resistance increased the likelihood of minor injuries, but not serious injuries, while both forceful and nonforceful verbal resistance decreased the likelihood of both minor and serious injuries.

Another important question missing from large-scale research is the frequency with which people are criminalized for resisting. We don't have large-scale studies to answer this question, but some resources created by community activists provide key insights into the issue. In their groundbreaking 2022 study, *Defending Self-Defense: A Call to Action by Survived & Punished*,[13] the UCLA Center for the Study of Women collaborated with abuse survivors who faced criminalization and incarceration for protecting themselves. Survivors, almost all of whom were women of color or queer and trans people of color, participated in a collaborative research project that demonstrated the barriers that highly targeted survivors face.

The report found that the most stigmatized survivors were put in an impossible position: they couldn't get help from the police or social service agencies. Because they couldn't trust the institutions that were supposed to help them, the violence escalated to the point where their lives were in danger. And because their lives were in danger, they had no choice but to hurt or kill the person who was abusing them. Some survivors couldn't call the police because they were involved in criminalized activities like sex work or drug use. Other times racist and transphobic violence that they or their communities had experienced in the past kept them from trusting the police. Social service agencies, including rape crisis and domestic violence programs, were also out of reach because they were seen as being too connected to the police or child protective services that sometimes take custody of kids because they blame the abused parent for "neglecting" the children.

A zine put out by the Oakland-based group TransFighters called *A Self-Defense Study Guide for Trans Women: Because the Stuff that Works for Other People Doesn't Work for Us* illustrates how some of the most targeted communities (for both violence and criminalization) have fewer options for resisting.[14] From the lived experience of community members, the zine explains how strategies that are seen as self-defense in cisgender women are likely to be read as aggression if trans women use them. In describing interactions ranging from abusive or transphobic family members to DMV workers giving someone a hard time about their gender marker on official documents, the zine says, "If you just stand up for yourself you could get punished in ways you can't defend yourself from." Instead, TransFighters advocate tactics like using cleverness to try to embarrass the person rather than yelling or speaking up. "Using aggressive body language will open the door for them to use their power to 'justifiably' punish you, so try victim body language instead." Noting that bystanders and court proceedings go against trans people more often than not, the zine authors advise enforcing physical boundaries in ways that can't be read as forceful. Rather than slapping someone who tries to grope you in a bar, for example, the zine presents subtle physical techniques to escape tight physical proximity. "Running from a fight is the best way to survive it," the zine advises.

Resistance is under-researched, but almost all the evidence shows that it makes people safer. That said, even effective resistance is not 100 percent effective. Because of this, it's important to honor and acknowledge that everyone does what they need to do to get through an act of violence. There is no guarantee that our own actions will stop an assault, but we are not wholly powerless either. The idea that compliance is the safest (or the only) option mostly benefits the people who rely on our compliance. Also, some evidence shows that feminist self-defense is beneficial even when it can't be used to stop every assault. Research by psychologists Lindsay Orchowski, Christine Gidycz, and Holly Raffle found that women who experienced sexual assault after having taken a feminist self-defense class had lower levels of self-blame than other survivors.[15]

ACTION STEPS

For Yourself

- When it comes to past experiences of sexual assault, trust yourself and honor yourself. Someone put you in an untenable position and you did what you could in that moment.
- Know that while the research is not complete enough to answer every question, it is relatively consistent in its finding that resistance stops assault, so don't let someone talk you out of your capability. If you hear a blanket statement that "fighting back doesn't work," particularly for sexual assault, know that all the available research shows the opposite.
- If you are faced with sexual coercion, sexual assaults, or someone you know trying to push past your sexual limits, know that fighting back is a viable choice. IMPACT Boston did a survey of college women who took our class in their senior year of high school. They were asked an open-ended question about whether they had thought about the self-defense class when they got to college. Here are two responses:

  > *"A guy was very intoxicated and was pulling me back to his room by grabbing viciously on my arm and basically dragging me (his room was down the hall from an extremely loud party, so I saw all of the problems there, for example no one would hear me yell etc.). Once we got to the room I told him I didn't want to do anything and I made sure to stay by the door and try to keep the door open. I thought back to all of the strategies I learned in IMPACT in case I needed to use them. I used my words to escape*

the situation once he tried to physically get me to do thing[s] with him and they thankfully worked so I didn't have to use force. The program allowed me to escape that situation safely and helped me recognize the signs of it potentially happening from the beginning."

"[We] were drunk, him more than me, and I did have to use physical force, using a groin slap, which I don't think I could have done as effectively without the program, or have been able to even think straight in that situation."

For Social Change

- Push for government and private funding of research on resistance that focuses on communities that are the most targeted for abuse and violence like Indigenous communities, queer and trans communities of color, and disabled communities. This research could also ask people about experiences of being criminalized or interrogated for using self-protection so we could understand on a large scale how that is different between the relatively privileged folks that are included in large-scale studies.
- If you are a statistician, mathematician, or any other person with the skills to analyze data, analyze the incident reports from the last five to ten years of NCVS data. The raw data is available to the public. The more we know about resistance, the better equipped we will be to keep ourselves and our communities safe.

PART 2

WHAT (OR WHO) TO FEAR

MYTH 3

"I READ IN THE NEWS THERE'S AN ATTACKER ON THE LOOSE, SO I NEED TO BE MORE CAREFUL OUT THERE"

It was May 2022. The pandemic had entered its third year, and I was struggling to keep my organization relevant in a news cycle dominated by midterm elections and infection surges. The #MeToo movement had been so completely eclipsed that I was starting to fear that sexual violence would never be topical again. So, when a reporter from a TV station in Providence, Rhode Island, emailed to say she wanted to interview me about a recent rape, I fixed my hair and cleared my schedule. I made a list of talking points and angled my laptop so the piles of clutter on my desk wouldn't be visible when I logged on.

In the early hours of the previous morning, a college student had been raped by a stranger who came into her apartment through an open window. A news report quotes the police as saying they believe the same man broke into another woman's apartment the same way, but he left when she screamed. The rapist was at large, the report said, so the police urged "caution," which they didn't clearly define.[1]

I'd forgotten about the second woman, the one who screamed. It wasn't until I looked up the news story to corroborate my memory that I realized there had been a second woman. And while the reporter chose the word "scream," in my mind the second woman yelled. There is nothing the first woman should have done differently.

The rape is not her fault or responsibility. What's also true is that the second woman stopped a rape with something as primal and ordinary as her voice. And the police, instead of acknowledging effectiveness of a loud and powerful voice, urged every young woman in Providence to be cautious.

I've been getting calls like this from reporters for twenty years. There's a story they're trying to tell and a role I'm supposed to play in it. "Stranger attacker is on the loose, and this self-defense expert has five easy things you can do to avoid being a victim." But in May 2022, I was ready. Without minimizing or dismissing the trauma of a rape by a stranger who breaks in through a window, I wanted to refocus the local news-watching public on the statistical reality. Most rapes—between 80 and 90 percent—are perpetrated by familiar people. Because of this, it makes more sense to be vigilant about people in our lives who touch our bodies without our consent, disregard our limits and boundaries, or try to coerce us into doing things we don't want to do. There are practical steps we can take to interrupt sexual violence, I wanted to tell the reporter. And they didn't necessarily involve putting bars on our windows or forgoing the joys of being a young college student.

I got on Zoom, smiling and excited. A little too appreciative that the reporter—whose hair and makeup were more fixed than mine would ever be—chose me out of all the self-defense teachers on the internet.

What should women do? she asked me.

I couldn't let the word "should" go. I launched into my talking points. The reporter cut me off. I said something about how the rape was the responsibility of the person who broke that window, and that the college student and any other survivor didn't do anything wrong. There's nothing women *should* do, but there's a lot we *can* do. Make noise, set boundaries, speak up when someone is trying to coerce us, use a strong part of our bodies against a weak part of an attacker's.

Shouldn't women be more careful about leaving their windows open?

Not necessarily, I said, reiterating that less than 20 percent of rapes are committed by strangers, that putting bars over your bedroom window was not necessarily the most effective precaution. I wanted to interrupt the vicious cycle of women restricting their lives because of a superficial characteristic of a stranger rape that happened to be in the news. Because someone was raped through an open window and someone else was raped while she was jogging at six in the morning and someone else was raped while wearing a short skirt and someone else was raped in a bathroom of a club by guy who spiked the drink she left on a pool table. And eventually it becomes like a depressing Dr. Seuss book, *I would not, could not have a life.*

I could imagine women listening to the police and locking their windows on a humid summer night. Tossing and turning with sweaty insomnia while men, who were not urged by the police to use caution, slept through the night with the help of a cross-breeze. I imagine how micro-disadvantages like this one add up. The next day at work, the woman is tired and unfocused while the man with whom she's competing for a promotion is rested, unaware of the college student whose rape made the news.

The reporter tried again. *Shouldn't women be more careful about leaving their windows open?*

The interview turned into a tug-of-war. She pressed me. I repeated my talking points, my fist clenched around the piece of paper I'd written them on. *People we know are more likely to sexually assault us than strangers*, I told her for probably the eighth time.

She was pleasant enough when she ended the interview, but she never returned my emails and the station never put me on the air.

I had a similar experience the following summer, with a Boston reporter. A man who had raped a couple of women in a neighborhood that is known as a tourist destination was at large, and she wanted me to tell women to clutch their keys and not walk alone after dark. Again, I talked about sexual assault by familiar people. When I saw the story online, the only sound bite she included was me saying that my organization was seeing an increase in demand for self-defense classes.

I've had some great experiences with thoughtful, responsible journalists over the years. But too often the kind of news story that drives interest in personal safety is a mismatch for the realities of sexual violence.

Local news plays a unique role in shaping people's opinions about violence, safety, and crime. People trust it more than national news. A 2024 Pew Research Center poll found that people across the political spectrum are highly satisfied with local news.[2] Seventy-one percent of respondents said they believe local media reports stories accurately, and 68 percent said local media covers the most important stories. This is markedly higher than a Pew study of all news media, which found that only 41 percent of people believe the media as a whole are covering the most important stories and 35 percent who say the media are reporting the news accurately.[3] The 2024 Pew survey also found that crime is second only to weather as a reason people turn to local news, with 77 percent of respondents saying they rely on local media for information about crime.

Despite widespread public trust in local news, research shows it misrepresents the realities of violence and crime. Sociologist Andrew J. Baranauskas analyzed three years of crime stories that appeared in the *Boston Globe*. He found that when compared to official Boston Police Department crime data, robberies and assaults in majority-white, higher income neighborhoods were significantly overreported compared to their actual prevalence. He also found that the *Globe* overreported homicides in Mattapan, a neighborhood that is 77 percent Black, while it underreported homicides in Dorchester, a racially mixed neighborhood that has high rates of poverty but is also 31 percent white.[4]

The decline in local news is well documented. Its effects include everything from decreased knowledge of political issues to less competitive local elections.[5] The problem gets worse when large corporations buy up local TV stations and severely curtail journalists' independence. Political scientist Matthew Levendusky conducted a systematic study of towns where the local news station is owned by Sinclair Broadcasting, a conservative media company. Sinclair-owned stations cover more national politics than a typical local news station—25 percent more national news than other local stations—and do so with a right-wing bias.[6] Sinclair also produces "must-run" segments that local stations are required to air, a practice that according to a 2018 *LA Times* investigation, and an anonymous open letter published on *Vox*, was vigorously opposed by reporters who argued that this type of requirement violated their journalistic ethics.[7]

Sinclair's footprint is outsized. Almost 40 percent of US households are located in cities and towns where the local news was owned by Sinclair. To examine the impact of this takeover of local TV news, Levendusky used Gallup poll data to assess changes in public opinion in zip codes where Sinclair acquired local TV news stations. Looking at the ten-year period between 2008 and 2018, he assessed changes in the political opinions of people whose local news was taken over by Sinclair during those years. He found no significant changes in people's party affiliations or self-identification as liberal or conservative, but he did find significant increases in the number of people who disapproved of Barack Obama. The effects were stronger for lower income voters and those with less formal education. Levendusky also found a modest but statistically significant change in voting patterns—6 percent of viewers who lived in zip codes where Sinclair acquired local news stations in that period and who had previously voted Democratic told Gallup they were not likely to vote for a Democrat for president. What's telling is that Levendusky found no effects on state and local elections. He attributes this to the fact that Sinclair broadcasts are standardized and focus more on national than local politics. While these numbers are modest, they are more than enough to win a presidential election in most swing states. And since people trust local news more than national news, Sinclair's strategy is having its intended effect.

Local news can influence people's beliefs about crime as well as their opinions about politics. Sociologists Andrew Baranauskas and Kevin Drakulich analyzed data from the American National Election Studies, a nationally representative survey that asks about media consumption and beliefs about a range of political issues.[8] They found that people who watched local TV news and crime dramas were more likely than others to support punitive crime policies. They also found that support for tough-on-crime policies was highest among white people who live near large populations of Black people. Though they are careful not to make causal inferences based on correlations, Baranauskas and Drakulich emphasized that print and online news did not have a significant effect on these opinions while local TV news did. Another unexpected finding was that national news outlets with explicit political slants like Fox and MSNBC did not move the needle on people's beliefs about crime the way that local news that is less overt in its political biases did.

The research reveals a complicated and sometimes contradictory picture of media coverage of sexual violence and how it affects our opinions. One study led by criminologist Meghan Sacks examined the top circulating local newspaper from each US census tract.[9] The study found lower rates of victim-blaming statements (like the victim was "asking for it" or that the alleged perpetrator was "not that kind of guy") in local news stories than in previous studies of national papers. Still, more than half the stories, 56 percent, were about stranger assaults, and articles were more sympathetic when survivors were injured or when the assault involved weapons or other severe violence.

Other research found persistent victim blame, even in local papers thought to be politically liberal. A series of studies led by psychologist Claire Gravelin shows a specific and immediate impact of exposure to victim-blaming news coverage.[10] In contrast to other research that used Gallup polls to measure public opinion without being able to determine whether the people who responded to Gallup had seen specific stories, Gravelin's team randomly assigned people to read different news stories and then measured their opinions about sexual assault. A series of three experiments systematically established the relationship between how local news outlets present sexual violence and the opinions of the people who read these stories.

In the first experiment, they analyzed differences in sexual assault coverage between the liberal-leaning *Boston Globe* and the conservative-leaning *New York Post*. Despite both papers' reputations for political biases in opposite directions, the analysis found more similarities than differences in their coverage of sexual violence. Both outlets overrepresented sexual violence by strangers—over 40 percent of the articles in both publications. Articles in both papers about acquaintance rapes were more likely than those about strangers to speculate about whether the victim was lying and to mention the victim's sexual promiscuity. The only significant difference they found between *Globe* and *Post* coverage was that 75 percent of *Post* articles about acquaintance rape included discussions of the victim's physical appearance, while none of the *Globe* articles did.

Participants in the second study were randomly assigned to read either a *New York Post* article about accused sexual abuser and football quarterback Ben Roethlisberger, which was deemed to be high in victim-blaming content, or an article written by the research team that addressed the same events but removed the victim-blaming statements.[11] One example of a statement the research team removed was "The accuser said her recollection of the details of the sex were hazy; she didn't know if Roethlisberger used protection."[12] After the research participants read the articles, they were asked questions designed to assess whether they agreed with victim-blaming statements, such as "How much is the alleged victim to blame for what happened?" and "How much do you think Ben took advantage of his alleged victim?"[13] They found that while the majority of people in all conditions—86 percent on average—understood the incident as rape, victim blame was higher among those who saw the *Post* article compared to the edited article. Victim blame was also higher among men than women across all conditions, a finding that is consistent with other research.

The third study demonstrates that reading news stories with victim-blaming content shapes people's opinions about sexual assault in general, not just the incident described in a particular article. Participants in this study were randomly assigned to read either the *Post* article or the version rewritten by the research team. But this time participants were asked not about Ben Roethlisberger but about an unrelated sexual assault scenario in which a woman reported having been raped by a man she'd met at a party while both were intoxicated. Those who were randomly assigned to read the *Post* article were more likely to blame the survivor in the hypothetical scenario than those who read the neutral article. This controlled experiment shows a direct and immediate impact of how victim-blaming news coverage affects our opinions. By putting people in a lab and randomly telling them which article to read, this study demonstrates that anyone's attitudes can be shaped. In contrast to studies that measure public opinion at a population level, it shows an immediate impact of exposure to a specific news story. People who choose to read the *New York Post* are likely drawn to that publication because it affirms their existing beliefs. But when people blame a survivor because they were told to read the *Post* in a laboratory, we realize just how vulnerable our beliefs can be.

While it's less researched, media coverage of women's resistance to rape and assault is just as important to understand. I think of the number of women and girls I've taught over the years who have burning questions about whether fighting back will make the attacker angry. It's a surprise to some when I say that resistance is effective. Even some groups that are savvy and unsurprised when I tell them most rapes are by familiar people are not aware that there is any research on what happens when we fight back.

Sociologists Jocelyn Hollander and Katie Rogers conducted the most comprehensive research on media coverage of women's resistance.[14] Their study, the only one of its kind that has been published, exposed some telling disconnects between what the research shows and what the news media reports. They analyzed a year's worth of articles in newspapers from every region of the US, including local and regional papers with small, midsize, and large circulations, as well as the *New York Times* and *USA Today*, the national outlets with the largest number of readers. They analyzed close to 1,000 articles (922 to be exact) that reported on a combined total of 1,084 incidents.

The study was inspired by a stark difference between a *Hartford Courant* article about a sexual assault of a University of Connecticut student and the student's own account of the assault, which was published in the campus newspaper. The *Courant* article described the student as hysterical and said that the assault stopped because a group of men came to her rescue. In the student's account, she describes fiercely resisting, hitting and kicking the assailants until they relented: "When he came toward me, I grabbed him by the shoulders and pushed him down to the ground. I held onto his shoulders and climbed on top to straddle him. He started thrashing side to side, but I was able to hit him with a closed fist, full force, in the face. A small crowd had gathered, mostly men. Now they seemed shocked. I was supposed to have been a victim, and I was breaking out of the mold."[15] Most women who survive violence that makes the news don't get to publish an account of their own experiences, so this is a rare and important example of how women's own experiences of their agency and power get erased. Hollander and Rogers systematically compared the media coverage to the evidence.

Citing then-current NCVS data, Hollander and Rogers note that 66 percent of women who reported being sexually assaulted also said they took some action to protect themselves. A much lower percentage of the news stories they analyzed—only 26.6 percent—mention any kind of resistance. Fewer than 15 percent described any kind of active resistance. More concerning is that the *New York Times* and *USA Today* were less likely than local and regional papers with smaller circulation to include any mention of women actively resisting—only 13.6 percent of national articles compared to 35 percent of those published in local papers.

As is not unusual for media coverage of sexual violence, incidents involving strangers were overrepresented. Just over half the articles included in the study were about stranger sexual assault. But Hollander and Rogers also found that when the assailant was a stranger, the article was more than twice as likely to acknowledge that the woman resisted. Of the articles that mentioned successful resistance, 60 percent were about strangers, 24 percent were acquaintances, and 16 percent were family members.

They also found that the power of women's resistance was consistently minimized. "When articles did report women's resistance, the power of those actions was frequently diluted by the way they were described. For example, reporters often wrote that resistance or escape was something women 'managed' to do, implying that it was not easy and that women were lucky, rather than skillful."[16] By contrast, descriptions of unsuccessful resistance were vivid. The research report includes several examples of articles that include graphic details of rapes and assaults. One article read, "According to [the police], [the assailant] tried to pull the woman toward the river. When she resisted and began to scream, he choked her and repeatedly punched her in the face before flinging her to the ground behind the bushes."[17] Another read, "She decided to become submissive, worried that he had a weapon and he'd kill her. . . . A hammer and a razor blade—tools she had used when moving into the apartment—were on her nightstand during the attack. But she couldn't reach them during those two hours. 'I just felt so useless,' she said."[18]

Also, while it might be intuitive to assume that longer articles would be more likely to include detailed descriptions of women's resistance, Hollander and Rogers found just the opposite. Feature-length stories were less likely to mention resistance than short crime reports. "Longer articles not only more frequently report women's submission," the authors note, "they also include additional detail that focuses on women's submission and fear." Longer articles also included more descriptions of bystanders who came to women's aid.

Shorter articles used more active language. Women were described as "fighting" rather than "struggling." Resistance was even more absent from headlines. Only 5 out of 922 headlines described a woman actively stopping an assault.

I wish there were more studies as comprehensive, systematic, and illuminating as this one. I wish, too, that someone would apply Claire Gravelin's study design to media coverage of women's resistance. I wonder if women would be less likely to assume they had no options if they saw more examples of women protecting themselves.

It doesn't have to be this way. Local news producers can generate the controversy they need to get clicks and views without reinforcing the myth that women are incapable of being our own protectors. I was fortunate to be part of one such news story. It was November 2017, only about a month after the #MeToo hashtag went viral.

The previous night, a woman in Cambridge, Massachusetts, had been attacked by a stranger. She fought back and got herself free, but the police issued an advisory—just for women—telling us never to wear earbuds or walk alone after dark.[19] It was November in the Northeast, where it starts getting dark before 5 p.m.

Instead of uncritically amplifying the police, reporter Carolyn Connley interviewed Cambridge women who were "rolling their eyes" at this advice. While the press release from the Cambridge Police described the woman as a "victim" who "was able to free herself from the suspect and ran away," the women of NBC News described her as having "fought off" the man. They interviewed women who were blunt in their assessment of the police department's advice, describing it as "victim blaming" and unrealistic to follow, noting too that the police should do their jobs and prevent crime rather than telling women to lock ourselves up. They interviewed me, and I talked about the lack of evidence to support the claim that wearing earbuds or walking around in the evening was any more dangerous than getting behind the wheel of a car. (And yes, they cautioned against earbuds with no evidence that the woman was wearing them!) All but the first two minutes of the story have disappeared from the internet forever. But the feeling of liberation I experienced when I watched the segment is something I will never forget. I took a particular delight that evening when I left my office after dark, wearing earbuds, listening to music, walking to the subway by myself. Feeling unconstrained by men who would try to make me scared of my daily routine.

ACTION STEPS

For Yourself

- Don't feel compelled to change your life because of the superficial characteristics of a stranger rape that makes the news. Open windows didn't become dangerous overnight just because one person used them to get into someone's apartment. Having self-defense skills can give you options in those types of situations. Being able to handle the unexpected can mean that you don't have to go to great lengths to alter your life. (Remember, that summer in Providence, the attacker left because the woman yelled.)
- At the same time, if locking your windows makes you feel safer, do it and don't blame or second-guess yourself. If there are a series of assaults in your community that take place in a similar location, it can be helpful to adjust your life to avoid that location if doing so is possible. But again, good self-defense training that gives you the skills to protect yourself in the moment of threat and intimidation will probably serve you better.
- Pay attention to whether the media you read or watch is shaping your opinions. Given that reading victim-blaming news stories changed people's opinions in a controlled study, it's useful to think about what media we consume and how it shapes our beliefs.

For Social Change

- If you see a news article that diminishes or minimizes women's resistance, write a letter to the editor of the paper or reach out to your local news station. Either that or use your own social media to challenge the publication to do better.
- Find out if your local news station is owned by Sinclair or another right-wing media corporation. If it is, educate people in your community about the ways they have blurred the lines

between opinion and reporting, and forced journalists to make public statements that support Sinclair's beliefs.

- If you have a local paper that is truly independent, subscribe and signal boost them. If not, subscribe to nonprofit news organizations.
- If people in your community have a sudden concern about sexual violence because of a news story about a stranger rape, see if you can get them to expand their attention to include a broader commitment to sexual violence prevention efforts. If there are widespread sexual abuse crises in schools or religious institutions in your community, this could be a good time to motivate people to hold the leaders of those institutions accountable. Your local rape crisis center may be launching prevention campaigns that you could amplify.
- If you are a researcher, replicate the Hollander and Rogers study so we can see if there are any changes in crime trends over time. Better yet, apply Gravelin's design so you can see whether news coverage affects people's opinions about women resisting sexual violence.

MYTH 4

"TREAT ANYONE WHO LOOKS OUT OF PLACE WITH SUSPICION"

"Any behavior that doesn't fit in and deviates from the landscape or crowd should be noted," says Steve Kardian, author of *The New Superpower for Women*. "Other things that should draw your attention include leering, someone talking to themselves in an overly animated way, or a person who is unduly watchful or nervous, their eyes rapidly darting back and forth. This could be a person looking for an opportunity to commit a crime."[1]

Or it could be an autistic person.

"There are some disabled people that will look nervous even if they're fine," says Zoe Gross, the director of policy and advocacy for the Autistic Self-Advocacy Network (ASAN). In an interview she explained, "This may be because of stimming that looks nervous to other people or because of a facial expression that appears strange, but it's just the way their face rests." Stimming, or self-stimulating, is a behavior that helps some autistic people manage sensory overload. Stimming behaviors differ, but often include repetitive actions like rocking, flicking a rubber band, or staring at an object.[2]

"Some autistic people in particular, our body language, and facial expression doesn't match what other people would expect," Zoe says. "So we can't be read as accurately by neurotypical people who look at us and think, 'Oh, that's an angry person,' but we're not angry or, 'Oh, I see that person is sad,' but we're not sad." Someone can look nervous when they're not. Or an autistic person could be nervous or stressed if they are more affected than a neurotypical person by a loud noise or a long line. This becomes a problem, Zoe says, when someone being different makes them appear suspicious. "We have an idea in our society," she explains, "that if you're acting in a way that differs from social norms, you're doing something that's morally wrong, and transgressive. And because of that, it may be more likely that you're going to do a dangerous thing."

Individual prejudices against autistic people are a problem, Zoe tells me, but ASAN is more concerned about those prejudices becoming the official policy of an organization or government entity. She gives Amtrak as an example. "If you go to an Amtrak station and they're playing their little safety video about what to watch out for," she says, "they talk about people who look nervous." A video put out by the Amtrak police lists the types of behavior passengers should "watch out for."[3] It includes "anyone loitering, staring, or watching employees and customers for a long period" and "anyone seeming nervous or acting in a disturbing manner" and "anyone taking notes or drawing diagrams while observing regular station activities." None of us are at our best when we're traveling, Zoe explains, and some autistic people are especially affected by changes in their routine. So they may look nervous, and they may be looking around in a way that seems like staring.

"You don't want to increase the possibility of police encounters with a marginalized group," Zoe explains. "And this does." It's hard to systematically track the relationship between stigma that equates autism or other disabilities with suspicion and police violence. In a position paper about police violence against disabled people, the Ruderman Family Foundation notes that part of the problem is that there is no legal requirement for law enforcement organizations to track or publish information about the number of incidents of police violence against disabled people.[4] That said, some of the most well-known Black people who were killed by police or died in police custody, including Sandra Bland and Freddie Gray, were also disabled. Also, federal data show that disabled people, particularly those who received special education services in school, are overrepresented in the US prison population.[5]

Zoe described a number of situations in which ASAN members were brought to the attention of the police. One person was stimming and encountered police officers who believed they were on drugs. "That can lead to violence, like tackling or restraining of the person; it can lead to a negative interaction where the person doesn't understand the instructions that are being given. And the police perceive that as defiance, or as they're about to run away and go to restrain them or escalate with them. We know of cases where autistic people have really negative reactions to interactions with law enforcement. In one case, we had an individual who lashed out in fear and injured an officer who tried to grab him—and, you know, he was jailed. Anything that's out there in the culture that is increasing the likelihood of police encounters is not great for us," Zoe explains.

In addition to the trauma of being incarcerated, a criminal record can make someone ineligible for employment, public housing, and even some social services. Criminalizing people for not responding to stress like neurotypical people can have serious and lasting effects.

Large-scale research on the impact of ableist ideas about suspicious behavior doesn't exist, but smaller studies shed light on the safety fears that autistic people and their caregivers have. For example, a 2020 study of 225 parents and professional caregivers of autistic people found that most were afraid of interactions with the police. This was true for 60 percent of the sample as a whole, but for those caregivers whose loved one had previous experience of interacting with the police, 77.7 percent reported fear of future interactions. In response to open-ended questions that asked those who responded "yes" to explain what they feared, the research team found three main categories: that their loved one would be misunderstood, that they could not communicate in a "reciprocal" or "prosocial" way when they were under the stress of interacting with a police officer, and that their loved one would respond to the stress in a way that a police officer would interpret as aggressive. It's worth noting that the majority of these caregivers have loved ones who are white, and whose average age at the time of the study was 40.

A 2022 qualitative study of police officers' self-reports of their interactions with autistic people by psychologist Lauren Gardner found discrepancies between Florida law and the officers' experiences.[6] Gardner notes that the state of Florida mandated autism training for police officers starting in 2017 after Miami police officer Jonathan Aledda shot and then handcuffed Charles Kinsey, a behavioral health worker who is Black.[7] Kinsey was supporting an autistic person who was carrying a toy fire-truck that Aledda said he believed was a gun. Despite this law, fewer than half the people Gardner surveyed had received autism training.

Gardner's team asked open-ended survey questions of 229 Florida police officers who were attending a training about autism, 130 of whom reported having interacted with a person they knew to be autistic. Of those officers, 37 percent were women, even though only about 10 percent of police officers in Florida are women. The survey asked officers to describe both their most recent interaction with a person they knew to be autistic and the most stressful encounter they had in the last twelve months. They found that the majority of calls were for incidents that were disruptive but not aggressive (47 calls). One example of this type of behavior was "showing a large sum of money in public." The second most common was the autistic person being the victim of abuse or neglect (43 calls), and the third was the autistic person being aggressive to themselves or others. Just over half the officers reported that, in their most recent calls, they spoke to the person or family and offered referrals to medical or other services.

That said, in a quarter of the most recent calls and 44 percent of the most serious calls, the officers responded by handcuffing, arresting, or involuntarily committing the autistic person to a psychiatric hospital. The authors note that the Florida law that gives police officers authority to require someone to undergo a psychiatric evaluation without their consent explicitly states that developmental disability alone is not a justification for invoking it. That said, some officers in this study said that involuntary commitment was a better option than incarceration when an autistic person exhibited aggressive behaviors that were dangerous to themselves or others. In this small sample, Gardner's team found that women officers were less likely to handcuff, arrest, or involuntarily commit autistic individuals than male officers.

In a follow-up study, Gardner's team found that formal training that included virtual reality and role-play simulations for interacting with autistic people increased officers' knowledge and confidence.[8] But Laurie Gardner says she is not aware of any published research that shows that police training actually improves officers' interactions with autistic people in the field.

The criminalization of difference, Zoe tells me, shows up in many areas of autistic peoples' lives, including colleges and universities. Even well-meaning administrators, who are trying to prevent everything from mass shootings to dating violence to suicide, can fall into ableism if Student of Concern policies are not clear about the difference between behavior that is threatening and behavior that nondisabled people find uncomfortable. Student of Concern policies provide a mechanism (usually an online form) to report someone who is behaving in ways that could indicate that they are a danger to others or in serious distress. Zoe tells me about people in the ASAN community who have been reported to college administrators for a range of behaviors. "It can be the way the student acts like speaking too loudly or quietly," she says. "Or maybe even something that can be triggering for legitimate reasons like not being aware of personal space." Student of Concern policies are important, but Zoe warns, "it can start to shade into reporting someone for signs of their disability. And then that, again, increases the likelihood that the student would be asked to leave the campus or be suspended or come to the negative attention of the campus administration." Zoe tells me about one college student who was reported because he paced up and down the hallways in his dorm.

Having early intervention policies to prevent mass shootings is one of the most important areas of progress in preventing gun violence in the United States. Reporter Mark Follman followed a group of FBI and forensic specialists who collaborate with psychologists and other service providers to identify people who are at risk of causing mass violence.[9] These teams provide skilled psychological services and social supports as well as emergency interventions to remove firearms or refer people whose actions are especially risky to psychiatric evaluation.

Based on detailed research of past mass shootings, FBI and psychological experts have identified risk factors for mass violence. "These include an obsession with weapons, a fixation on images of violence, and a history of aggressive acts that aren't directly related to the planned attack—possibly a way for the perpetrator to test his resolve," Folman reports. Other risk factors include an unshakable sense of grievance that stirs thoughts about harming other people (for example, 2014 mass shooter Elliot Rodger was aggrieved that women wouldn't date him). Analysis of journals and online activity of mass shooters have found that these acts may appear spontaneous but are almost always methodically planned. In the planning process, Follman notes, most shooters reveal their intentions in small ways. Experts call this "leakage." Sometimes, a person planning a mass shooting posts videos or rants on social media declaring their intentions to commit violence. Other times, they make comments about killing people to friends. Others talk about their admiration for past mass shooters.

These are specific behaviors, informed by thorough analysis of evidence. When threat assessment teams get diverted by behaviors that are thought to be "weird," it not only stigmatizes autistic people but pulls them away from situations where they are needed. Many Student of Concern policies, in their effort to be comprehensive, wind up being vague. Emerson College encourages people to make a report about any student that is "exhibiting behavior that is disruptive, worrisome, or poses a potential threat to the safety and well-being of the campus community."[10] The Florida State policy includes "unusual behavior" and "disrupting the classroom, event, or normal business operations."[11] Not all Student of Concern policies are vague. Some, like those of the University of Nebraska at Lincoln, have clear definitions of a wide range of concerning behaviors ranging from abusing a dating partner to financial stress to suicidal thoughts. The Student of Concern policy is also explicit in directing students not to diagnose students or jump to conclusions about their conditions.[12]

There are good reasons to make a reporting process as accessible as possible. But if that is the case, the people who receive the reports and decide how to address them need to be skilled and knowledgeable about autism and other differences so that they are not conflating autistic students with students at risk to harm others.

Zoe invites us to challenge the belief that the police are a neutral party, or that they have the patience and expertise to distinguish between an unfamiliar but harmless behavior and signs of threat. "People think, 'Well, I thought this person was acting suspicious. So I'll call the police,'" she says. "And if nothing is going on, then nothing bad will happen. And then if they really are on drugs, or have a gun, then the police will do something that I deem appropriate, and then that'll all be fine. But what may happen is that nothing is going on, and the police do something that you wouldn't deem appropriate, and it's not all fine. I think if more people knew about that, fewer people would call the police."

One of the most egregious examples of this inability or unwillingness to distinguish between danger and difference happened in 2014, when Kayleb Moon-Robinson, then an eleven-year-old Black autistic boy, was charged with crimes for kicking a trash can in his sixth-grade classroom.[13] Kayleb was in his first year of middle school, still struggling to get used to a new building, and having to change classrooms multiple times during the day. He was having trouble getting from one classroom to another because changes in his routine were difficult for him.

In an interview with Morénike Giwa Onaiwu, a Black autistic woman who is a disability rights activist, she explains how school staff set Kayleb up for failure and then criminalized him for getting frustrated. He had a hard time changing classrooms, so the teachers made him wait for an aide to escort him. When he tried to leave class with the other kids, they stopped him. He kicked a trash can, so they called the school resource officer. The officer grabbed Kayleb to bring him to the principal's office. Kayleb has a hard time being touched, so he struggled. The officer, according to Kayleb's account, "slammed me down and then handcuffed me." The officer then charged him with felony assault against a police officer and disorderly conduct. A follow-up investigation by the Center for Public Integrity found that Virginia, where Kayleb lives, was at the time more likely than any other US state to involve children with the police in schools.[14]

In response, Morénike and fellow activist Lei Wiley-Mydske launched a Change.org petition to draw attention to Kayleb's situation and get the charges dropped. Morénike lives in Texas and had never met Kayleb or his family. But as a Black autistic woman with two children who are also autistic, she was horrified when she heard what the police had done. "I could easily see that being one of my kids," she said. Kayleb was a small child, she thought. He'd been formally diagnosed with autism and had an Individualized Education Program (IEP) that specified he needed help with transitioning from one classroom to another. Morénike, who has a master's degree in special education, notes that by not following Kayleb's IEP, the school was disregarding the law.

Morénike notes that the social stigma the school staff put on Kayleb set him up for this outburst. "He had, like a lot of autistic children, difficulties with transition. Kind of gets distracted, or are slower," she says. "So I guess he was moving a little more slowly than they thought. And so their idea, instead of utilizing some of the tools in the IEP to help him with transitions, or let him leave early, or whatever their decision was, they were going to have him wait when everybody else leaves the class. The bell rings. Everybody else leaves, he has to stay there and wait for an aide to come get him, and then trail him to the next class, wherever it was, on another floor, or whatever, and then get him situated.

"Well, he's this sixth-grade child. He's embarrassed by that. He doesn't want to be othered like that. That's the whole reason why you mainstream children, so they can have interactions with their peers. And then there was a cute little girl that he likes, that he wanted to walk in the hall next to. And so he didn't." Morénike notes, "This plan was not in his IEP; this is something the school decided to do. They felt like they were being supportive or helpful. He felt like he was being othered."

Having worked in education, Morénike understands both the good intentions and the pressures facing the school staff. Also, she acknowledges that a lot of IEP information is not shared with everyone in the school, so the resource officer might not have realized Kayleb was autistic. "I don't think they were setting him up intentionally; I think that's what ended up happening," she says. "They did not follow his IEP for a child they don't know anything about." But Kayleb had thrived in elementary school, where teachers knew him and followed his IEP. She also sees the impact of this officer's actions causing trauma all around. For a kid to have a tantrum and in response see "someone throwing them to the ground, and pushing them down and handcuffing them in front of everybody and yelling at them, it's so humiliating," she says. "And traumatizing for the other children to watch as well."

Also, she tells me, Kayleb was in an unusual situation as a Black autistic boy who came from a family of police officers. "Some other children in the Black community had maybe had that thing where you're told to watch police or be careful. But Grandpa's police. And Grandpa's parents are police. So he wasn't scared of police. He loved the police."

It was obvious to Morénike that this child needed help, not punishment, and that he posed no threat to the officer or anyone else. "I'm looking at this child thinking this kid was handcuffed," she tells me. "He's tiny. His voice hadn't changed yet. He is clearly disabled. I'm thinking, okay, so he kicked a trash can because he got frustrated. That's not [a] felony."

She wanted the media to pay attention to how egregious this was. She envisioned constituents flooding the inboxes of their representatives, and news stories with pictures of this small autistic boy who struggled against the confinement of handcuffs, and because of that was declared a criminal.

She was active on social media. There were communities she wanted to reach, like other parents of kids with disabilities who didn't face the added stigma of racism. "They didn't give him the benefit of the doubt that another child in a different setting would have gotten," she says. "Because of that, they saw a Black child not doing what they thought he should do, and they made a million assumptions that were wrong and that hurt him. That was one of the reasons why I pushed the petition so hard to so many communities. I pushed it to autism communities because I wanted people to see that this is what's happening, and so there were so many people who were nonblack. They were autism parents who were shocked because they were also realizing, 'Oh my gosh, this could happen to my child too. My child may not share the skin tone, but because of disability, their behavior can be misunderstood and they can be endangered.'" She also wanted to push it into Black communities because she wanted people to realize how racism intersects with ableism.

Morénike spent every spare moment bringing attention to Kayleb's case. *There's a lot of police violence we find out about too late*, she thought. But in his case, she could do something.

Morénike understood the complicated position Kayleb's mother, Stacy Doss, was in. In addition to defending Kayleb against criminal charges, Stacy was also being pressured to work out a deal that would have sent Kayleb to an alternative school, a proposal Morénike describes as nonsense and bullying. Morénike didn't want to speak for the family, but she realized she was in a better position to draw attention to the case than Stacy.

The petition got traction, going from a few hundred signatures to thousands in a short amount of time. On the day of Kayleb's court appearance, Morénike, in collaboration with ASAN, delivered it to the courthouse. By that time, it had over 150,000 signatures. And it wasn't just the signatures; most of the people who signed wrote comments. The comments that moved Morénike most were from people who knew Kayleb personally, who described him as a gentle, curious child. An elementary school teacher from Kayleb's previous school signed the petition. So did a neighbor.

Morénike flew to Virginia to attend Kayleb's hearing. She knew the courthouse was being inundated with phone calls and emails, but she wanted a visual representation of how many people had signed the petition. So, the night before the hearing, she went to a copy store to print it out. There were so many pages that she needed a store employee to help her carry the huge pile of paper to her car. She bought a wagon later that night so she could wheel the petition to the courthouse.

Morénike, ASAN, and other supporters held a press conference on the stairs of the courthouse and used it to bring attention to the situation. It attracted the media, which prompted the Center for Public Integrity to investigate the outsized role that police were playing in school discipline in Virginia.

Charges against Kayleb were dropped, and more scrutiny was given to the role of police in schools. Still, Morénike is careful not to be too rosy about the outcome. "Ultimately, I do feel like it was a victory," she tells me. But the price for Kayleb and his family was too high. "It stole his innocence. That's heartbreaking for any kid that age to have to suddenly know how terrible the world is when you're eleven or twelve."

But she knows that Black autistic people are too easily criminalized when their behaviors or facial expressions don't make sense. And the change happens because a Black autistic mother in a state a thousand miles away feels a deep sense of urgency. Morénike believes that most civil rights victories we read about in history books begin this way. "It's some little person who decided to say or do something and made a change," she says. "And so the family shouldn't have had to fight that fight alone. And I don't think that they would have had the outcome they did, if not for the public scrutiny."

We need to have clarity and discernment when we see behaviors that are unfamiliar or make us uncomfortable. If we don't, the consequences could be anything from social exclusion to violence. Equating difference or stigma with danger is not only bad for people who are targets of that stigma; it is also bad for people with relative privilege, especially young middle-class women whose most likely experience of violence is sexual assaults from people they know. If we teach our daughters to associate threat cues with outsiders, then we leave them unprepared for the guys they date or go to parties with. Guys who are charming and socially adept when they dismiss a girl who says "no" or hesitates or doesn't say and unambivalent "yes" to whatever kind of sex the charming boy wants. If she's taught that a threatening person is a creepy outsider, she won't recognize sexual coercion soon enough.

A person on the other end of a subway platform who is swearing, yelling, and ranting to himself, but not paying me any attention, is less of a threat to me than a person who is charming and complimenting me while they move closer, and ignoring me when I say I don't want to talk. One may make me viscerally uncomfortable, but if I apply discernment, I am clearer about the difference between threatening behavior and my own discomfort.

A person who is homeless or intoxicated in public is not a threat to me just because they are sitting or lying on a sidewalk, and maybe they smell like alcohol or they haven't showered in a while. In the self-defense classes IMPACT Boston teaches, we present a scenario that takes place at a subway station. A person starts by standing too close to me. I move away. He then strikes up a conversation and asks for directions. But when I say I don't know where the street that he's looking for is, he keeps talking to me. I tell him I don't want to talk, then pay attention to what he does. We want students to recognize that the threatening behavior is dismissing my limits, getting close to me and continuing the conversation when I've already said "no," not looking or acting "strange."

A person stimming on an elevator is not a threat to me. A person who stands right next to me in an otherwise empty elevator, and moves closer to me when I move away, is crossing my boundaries. If I give that person the benefit of the doubt and firmly but respectfully ask for more space, I can get a clearer idea of whether they have problems with social interactions or whether they pose a threat. A person who looks away when they speak to me or has an unfamiliar facial expression is not necessarily a threat.

ACTION STEPS

For Yourself

- Practice discerning the difference between behaviors that are unfamiliar or breaking social conventions from behaviors that are coercive or threatening. If someone has an unfamiliar facial expression or is making noises or moving their body in ways that are not comfortable or familiar, that is probably not a threat. If someone is, on the other hand, standing too close to you, or insisting they are entitled to your attention when you've already refused, or trying to overpower your boundaries, that is the actual "suspicious behavior."
- Get education about common stims and other behaviors that autistic people may use to manage the sensory overload of being in a public place, so you don't equate them with suspicious behavior.

For Social Change

- If you are part of a university or organization that has a Student of Concern policy, make sure it is consistent with the evidence about warning signs for violence or harm, and not just any behavior that makes any person uncomfortable. There are good reasons to make reporting as easy and accessible as possible. It makes sense to encourage students to error on the side of reporting. But if that's the policy, make sure the people receiving the reports have excellent training in racism and ableism (including how to differentiate implicit biases from actual threatening behavior) as well as a high level of knowledge about autism and other disabilities that impact the way people behave in public places or social situations. Also, do regular audits to ensure that those reported as "Students of Concern" are not disproportionately disabled or people of color. If they are, provide more explicit education about the difference between racial and disability bias and reasonable concern.

- If you see an encounter with police, record it.
- If you are a parent (whether your child is autistic or not), push for information about your school's relationship with the police. Push for explicit policies and standards about which types of discipline are handled by school counselors and teachers. Fight for published data about the race and disability status of students reported to school police.

MYTH 5

"CRIME IS AT AN ALL-TIME HIGH AND GOING UP"

The 2016 presidential election feels like it happened in the impossibly distant past. The capacity for disbelief I had back then, the confidence I had that any number of things were just not possible, feels no less remote than the supposed innocence of childhood. I remember how incredulous I was when Donald Trump and his supporters insisted that crime was at an all-time high.

I have a clear memory of a woman reporter trying to fact-check a Trump surrogate. The interview was filmed in a media booth at the Republican National Convention. It was daytime. The chairs that would be filled by ecstatic delegates later that night were mostly empty. A few people in bland suits wandered among the empty rows. In my memory, the Trump surrogate was Rudy Giuliani, though my efforts to find the clip were not successful. How could they be with the sheer volume of results that come up when you type "Giuliani," "Trump," "Crime," and "2016 election" into a search engine. But I clearly remember the man who might have been Rudy Giuliani repeating the false claim: *crime is going up*. The claim was made with a calculated hysteria that bled easily into the predictable demonizations: of immigrants, of cities, of Black Lives Matter activists. The reporter kept correcting the claim, as if it was a mistake and not a strategy. The surrogate was insistent, sometimes talking over the reporter. As if she wasn't there. As if she hadn't contradicted a key Trump talking point with facts. I turned off the TV, went back to my life, and convinced myself that come November, Trump would go back to being a reality TV star and a national joke.

I would have described myself as savvy and politically aware back then, and for the most part, I would not have been wrong. But for all the myths about safety and violence I debunked every day, my understanding of the deliberate forces behind this distortion was not nearly as sophisticated as the distortion itself.

Public opinion about crime is stubbornly out of touch with reality. In a 2023 Gallup poll, the number of people who said they believed crime was going up reached a record high of 77 percent.[1] Fifty-five percent of respondents said they believed crime in their own neighborhoods had increased in the previous year. Sixty-three percent said they believed crime was very or extremely serious, up from 54 percent in the previous poll in 2021. Beliefs about crime differed by political affiliation, but across the spectrum the people who believed correct information were in the minority. Seventy-eight percent of Republicans said they believed crime was very or extremely serious compared to 60 percent of independents and 51 percent of Democrats. Nearly all Republicans—92 percent—said they believed crime had increased in the previous year, compared to 78 percent of independents and 58 percent of Democrats.

It feels almost pointless to say this, but the evidence shows just the opposite. The Bureau of Justice Statistics publishes a report every year based on the results of the National Crime Victimization Survey. Most people with internet access can find it. The results are presented in a series of meaningful bullet points and are, for the most part, free of statistical jargon. Violent crime overall was lower in 2023 than it had been in 2022, with 23.5 victimizations per 1,000 people in 2022 compared to 22.5 per 1,000 people in 2023.[2]

The 2023 Gallup poll was not unique. In August 2024, the Pew Research Center published a deep dive into this disconnect.[3] They found that in twenty-three out of twenty-seven Gallup polls conducted since 1993, the year that crime in the US began its downward trajectory, 60 percent or more of respondents said that they believe that crime was going up. This study also found that people who get their information from local news have the highest level of concern about violent crime. They also found that even though property crime is more common in the United States than violent crime, survey respondents said they saw media coverage of violent crime at nearly the same frequency as they saw coverage of property crime.

Challenging misinformation or disinformation is more effective when we are clear about who benefits from the distortions. Restorative justice leader Zach Norris has a name for politicians, political consultants, and pundits who stoke our fear of crime to advance their agendas: "architects of anxiety," he calls them. In his book *Defund Fear*, Norris exposes the "fearmongers and the fear-profiters, people who manipulate our anxieties so we buy what they want us to buy and vote how they want us to vote."[4] Stoking the public's anxiety about crime, he argues, largely benefits conservatives with wealth and power.

As an example of both the deliberateness with which these architects manipulate our fear and the results it produces, Norris cites a speech given to fossil fuel industry executives in March of 2019 by then assistant secretary for land and minerals management Joe Balash. Balash told the executives that what he found thrilling about working in the Trump administration was the way the president could keep the attention of the media and the public focused elsewhere while his agency rolled back environmental protections and implemented corporation-friendly policies. "Almost every time that powerful interests mention 'bad guys' and outsiders who pose a threat to our families, our homes, and our way of life," Norris argues, "we should pause and consider the implications rather than allow a knee-jerk reaction based on our unconscious brain's hypervigilance to threats. With their smoke and mirrors, whom might the architects of anxiety be trying to protect, and whom are they blaming and scapegoating?"[5]

Mother Jones reporter Samantha Michaels documented how architects of anxiety succeeded at scaring people into opposing once-popular criminal justice reforms in the San Francisco Bay Area. Recall campaigns in Oakland and San Francisco unseated progressive district attorneys Chesa Boudin and Pamela Price, both of whom were blamed for less than factual crime spikes because they worked to end mass incarceration, addressed racial disparities in sentencing, investigated deaths of people held in jails, and tried to hold the police accountable for violence against community members. Homicides and shootings were truly increasing in Oakland at the time of Price's election and inauguration (though they were trending down again by the time the recall campaign started). But recall supporters also spread false information. On the Nextdoor app, false statements circulated about Price buying televisions for prison inmates.[6] Recalls of Boudin, Price, and Oakland Mayor Sheng Thao were bankrolled by wealthy hedge fund managers and amplified by public relations consultant Sam Singer, who counts the Oakland Police Union among his clients.[7] Singer denied having direct involvement in the recall campaigns that ultimately unseated Price and Thao, but he used his platform on X to raise alarm about crime rising in Oakland and to blame homeless people and progressive policies for causing it. This, despite the steep reductions in crime in 2023 that followed the pandemic-era spikes.

There is something visceral about fear for our bodily safety. It's urgent, it defies logic. It is stoked and manipulated in ways that other fears can't be. For people whose race and class insulate us from the most aggressive policing tactics, concepts like equity and accountability can become less compelling than anxiety about a crazed stranger killing someone we love. When we experience this urgent, powerful fear, we are easily convinced that it's naive to think crime could be solved by affordable housing or stable employment or abundant substance use services provided by people who know what they're doing. There are so many narratives about how idealistic people are misguided, and these get amplified every time an alternative to punishment produces less than perfect results. It can be tempting to see supporting the police as the only realistic, mature solution.

Author and civil rights lawyer Alec Karakatsanis analyzed how news media and police work together to shape our understanding of crime. Shifting our attention away from crimes like wage theft and violations of environmental laws that are committed by corporate executives, the news media instead focuses on robberies and low-level violence by poor people. (I would add that every handful of years, news media get interested in sexual violence, and there are some impressive changes in reporting on how organizational leaders cause harm by enabling abusers.)[8] In his *Copaganda* newsletter on Substack, Karakatsanis argues that "daily news is dominated by 'crime' stories. But even these are 'crime' stories of a certain kind: they aren't stories about the many corporate air pollution crimes, for example. Instead, they are the kind of 'crimes' publicized by police press releases, usually involving poor people. Much of deadly US water pollution is also criminal, but 'law enforcement' chooses to ignore it, and thus so do most journalists."[9] He cites Department of Justice data showing that in 2020, only twenty-three people were charged with environmental crimes compared to twenty-three thousand charged with drug and immigration crimes.

In February 2023, Karakatsanis published a roundup of investigations that found steep increases in public relations spending by police departments, often in the aftermath of outrage about police-involved killings. One such example was uncovered by Geoffrey Cubbage of the Better Government Association, a think tank focused on public policy and government spending in Illinois. Cubbage documented a dramatic increase in the public relations staff in the Chicago Police Department (CPD) after the murder of Laquan McDonald by Chicago police officer Jason Van Dyke: "The 2016 budget, which was prepared in 2015 while the Emanuel administration was fighting a public records request and subsequent lawsuit that eventually forced the release of the shooting footage, increased the police department's public relations team from six full-time employees to 25. Additional staff in the 2017, 2018 and 2019 budgets more than doubled CPD's communications staff to a peak of 52 full-time employees in Emanuel's last year in office."[10]

A 2020 *Los Angeles Times* investigation by journalist Maya Lau uncovered a similar trend in Southern California. Lau discovered that the Los Angeles County Sheriff's Department had 42 employees devoted to public relations and the Los Angeles Police Department had an additional 25. In 2015, a cell-phone video showed police shooting and killing Nicholas Robertson as he walked away from them. The video went viral and sparked protests. In response, the police department released their own video showing Robertson pointing a gun at the deputies. News media ran stories about the police video, and protests died down. But when the investigation was complete, it was clear that the information the police had released was not the full story. "Two years later, a more close-up video emerged that contradicted the deputies' claims," Lau reported. "Robertson did not point the gun at deputies just before the shooting, and the gun was not loaded." A jury that reviewed all the evidence, including the complete video, awarded $3.6 million to Robertson's family, citing the deputy's negligence.[11]

As Lau dug deeper into the public relations activity of the police departments in California, she found that this effort to shape public opinion in the wake of police-involved killings was not isolated. After a 2011 fatal beating of an unarmed homeless man in Fullerton, the police department began paying the PR firm Cornerstone Communications to maintain a website that included not only the police narrative of the killing but stories about valor ceremonies, winter coat drives, and other ways the police had helped the community. Departments in Southern California followed suit, leading to the creation of the website Behind the Badge, a police PR site developed by Cornerstone Communications and designed to look like a news site.[12] The firm's founder, Bill Rams, is a former reporter who worked for a local newspaper in Orange County.

In an interview with Lau, Rams noted that as local newspapers disappear, sites like Behind the Badge help the public understand the police. With decreasing options for other perspectives, Lau discovered, Californians' tax dollars were used to fund this police-approved narrative. Stories on Behind the Badge include heartbreaking tales from crime victims who thank the police for saving their lives, stories of brave officers who don't give up even when bad guys shoot at them, and feature articles on district attorneys who urge harsh punishments for looters. The site has also published stories about crime spikes and the public's fear of "lawlessness."[13] Lau's investigation found that departments were paying between $24,000 to $72,000 per year to be included in Behind the Badge. For this and for publishing a list of deputies whose actions were being scrutinized, Lau became the subject of a criminal investigation by the LA Sheriff's department, which was eventually closed with no findings.[14]

The strategy of using the news media to shape people's perceptions of the police has been around for decades. One example is a 2002 report by the Police Executive Research Forum, an advocacy and training organization for police chiefs and department leaders that has a history of both bolstering policing and advocating for commonsense reforms like de-escalation training. The report, titled *Media Relations and Police Budgeting: A Successful Equation*, urges police leaders to develop close relationships with local media.[15] It presents an analysis of police departments in Florida, Arizona, and North Carolina that built successful relationships with reporters, as well as a survey of investigative journalists about their experiences and concerns about covering law enforcement. The journalists said they wanted candor from the police, access to department leadership, and timely, useful information rather than feeling dismissed by public information officers who were not authorized to share anything substantive.

The report opens with an analysis of media coverage of the then-recent shooting of Amadou Diallo and abuse of Abner Louima by the New York Police Department. Noting that media coverage of those events damaged the police department's credibility, the report argues that this happened because most of the information given to journalists came from protesters, bystanders, victims, and local commentators, with very little coming directly from law enforcement officials.

The report recommends that police chiefs and high-ranking officers build relationships with reporters and be candid, even about the department's errors. "As media personnel grow more familiar with police department policy and routine activities, they gain a professional respect for law enforcement," the report asserts. "That respect leads to more favorable reporting, which ultimately improves public opinion of the police." This can mean feeding the reporters stories to help them on slow news days and getting together for informal lunches.

It ends with examples of how favorable media coverage leads to public support for increased funding, whether to contain mass protests or finance more mundane services. Getting a reporter to write a story about parents' concerns about speeding in school zones can translate to support for more officers patrolling near schools. The Charlotte-Mecklenburg Police Department invited the media to film and photograph semiautomatic weapons they had seized during a series of arrests. In a press conference, they displayed the criminals' weapons side by side with the weapons the police officers carried. "That press conference successfully demonstrated the department's urgent need for better firearms and the funds necessary to acquire them," the report asserts. "A news correspondent for WBTV in Charlotte recalled that the firearms display had a great impact on the media's and community's understanding of the importance of additional funding and ultimately helped the department obtain funds for upgrading its weapons."[16] It's clear that police agencies have taken this advice and invested taxpayer funds in producing news that portrays the police in a positive and emotionally accessible way. As just one example of this practice, journalist Radley Balko identified 30 videos from municipalities all over the country that featured police officers saving baby ducks.[17]

Karakatsanis makes an incisive argument about how our understanding of crime would be different if other municipal departments had the same opportunity to create news. "The content of daily news would be very different if, let's say, the local bureaucrats who test lead levels in water or workplace safety code violations had the same infrastructure and commitment to producing news and conventional wisdom. For example, imagine a daily news segment called 'bad landlord of the day' where local news simply reported on the worst eviction law or building code violations that government agencies document each day. Same for a 'bad employer of the week' segment for child labor or wage theft violations that local, state, and national regulators are finding every day."[18]

His analysis sheds light on the complex forces behind the intractable beliefs about crime that the Pew study uncovered. On the most basic level, it shapes the public understanding of what constitutes a "crime." In our imagination, it is one individual taking money from another or physically hurting them, not corporate executives making decisions that expose hundreds of employees to toxic chemicals.

One example of architects of anxiety divorcing public opinion from evidence was seen in New York State in the wake of bail reform legislation passed in 2019 (and amended several times over the next three years), which sought to decrease recidivism and racial disparities by prohibiting judges from setting bail for a defined set of misdemeanors and other nonviolent offenses. Rene Ropac and Michael Rempel of the Data Collaborative for Justice, a project of the City University of New York's John Jay College of Criminal Justice, conducted an analysis that compared those impacted by bail reform to similar defendants who were required to post bail or were incarcerated before their cases were adjudicated.[19] From sophisticated statistical analyses and thoughtful efforts to identify a comparison group that was truly similar to defendants impacted by bail reform, the project yielded nuanced but promising findings. For those with no prior arrest, being released under the terms of the new law resulted in lower recidivism by several measures: lower rates of overall rearrest (26 percent vs. 38 percent), lower felony rearrest (12 percent vs. 20 percent), and lower violent felony rearrest (6 percent vs. 10 percent). There was also a modestly lower rate of rearrest for firearm offenses. That said, the report also found that defendants who had a recent violent arrest and another pending case against them at the time of the arraignment were more likely to reoffend than similar defendants who were arrested (and incarcerated) before the law went into effect.

These findings could have informed nuanced public policy. It could have brought New York closer to balancing compelling public safety concerns with harms caused by incarcerating people who were still presumed innocent. Instead, New York mayor Eric Adams began lambasting bail reform on national and local news, and he did so by raising the profile of tragic crimes that were not relevant to the law. One such incident was a man who committed an assault with a baseball bat after he was released on bail.[20] Not only was the crime this man committed not included in the bail reform law, but the man was able to commit the subsequent crime because he was able to post cash bail.

A press release from Republican representative Elise Stefanik in 2023, a year when violent crime was going down after its Covid-era spikes, includes quotes from other politicians who agree with her efforts to roll back bail reform. They include this one from Congressman Andrew Garbarino: "Every single day violent crime is splashed across the front pages of New York newspapers. New Yorkers live in fear as crime rates continue to rise and our law enforcement officers fight to keep our communities safe while contending with reduced resources and state laws like cashless bail making their jobs harder."[21] This quote exemplifies the vicious cycle—the news media stokes fear of crime, politicians treat media coverage of that fear as if it were solid evidence, they create more news by stoking fear, and then people tell public opinion researchers that they believe crime is going up.

It's not just the news that divorces people's beliefs about crime from reality. Another powerful contributor to this problem is entertainment media. Not only are the police overrepresented in TV shows compared to every other profession, but there are deliberate efforts to portray them as the good guys and anyone working to hold them accountable as a corrupt or disingenuous nuisance. Most historians and journalists trace this state of affairs to the 1950s police show *Dragnet*. *Vox* culture writer Constance Grady notes that the earliest movies about the police portrayed them as bumbling and incompetent, like the Keystone Cops, which debuted in 1912.[22]

But that changed with the *Dragnet* series. Historian and MacArthur Fellow Mike Davis is one of the many academics and journalists to document the close relationship between Jack Webb, the show's producer who also starred as Detective Joe Friday, and the Los Angeles Police Chief William H. Parker. Parker not only made blatantly racist statements that Black people and Mexicans were less civilized and therefore predisposed to commit crimes, but he also succeeded at removing civilian oversight of the police in the 1930s, ensuring that all misconduct claims were handled exclusively by ranking officers. When *Dragnet* began production, Parker offered Webb unlimited cooperation and access to LAPD facilities if Webb agreed to get approval for all scripts from the department. Any storyline the police didn't approve was scrapped. In exchange, LAPD let Webb use police cars, film on city streets, and have officers as extras, lowering the costs of production and making the show more "authentic."

Grady gives a pointed example of how *Dragnet* diverged from reality: "In 1951, the same year that *Dragnet* premiered, multiple members of the LAPD assaulted seven civilians, leaving five Latino men and two white men hospitalized with broken bones and ruptured organs. Racially motivated violence against civilians was and still is part of the reality of the police force. But Webb and his collaborators at the LAPD deliberately elided that reality, giving us the fantasy of the hero cop instead."

Reporter Alyssa Rosenberg documented explicit efforts by movie industry executives to cultivate relationships with the Los Angeles police as a way to protect stars who were engaged in criminal activity as well as those whose careers would have been ruined if the public discovered that they were gay.[23] Following *Dragnet* were similar shows in the 1960s, *Highway Patrol* and *FBI*. Rosenberg notes that *FBI* aired at a time when J. Edgar Hoover was investigating Martin Luther King and other civil rights leaders, but the fictional characters were presented as morally pure. Television shows that are relentless in their positive portrayals of the police continue to this day. Dick Wolf, owner of the Law and Order franchise, is unapologetic about the pro-police message of the series.[24] His close relationships with the NYPD, including paid police consultants, is well documented.

A 2020 study led by the Racial Justice Advocacy Group Color of Change and the Annenberg Norman Lear Center at the University of Southern California[25] found that 60 percent of the prime-time shows on the largest television networks are about the police. In analyzing crime shows over time, they noticed some key changes. In the 1980s, defense lawyers were heroes. Though the characters were all white men (like Matlock and Perry Mason), criminal defense was depicted as noble, necessary work. Defense attorneys "once embodied the character of the American hero, defending the innocent against the many police officers, prosecutors and judges who jumped to conclusions too quickly and stood as symbols of a deeply flawed system," the report notes.[26]

But as the Law and Order franchise gained prominence in the 1990s and 2000s, portrayals of defense lawyers changed. They were no longer main characters who earned our empathy. They were devious and manipulative. They impeded our heroes and helped guilty people avoid punishment. And as portrayals of defense lawyers became negative, the report notes, more people of color were cast in these roles, sometimes underhandedly obstructing prosecutors and detectives, other times explicitly playing the "race card" to divert attention from the facts of the case.

The Color of Change study reviewed 353 episodes of 26 popular TV shows. In addition to crime dramas overrepresenting cities and underrepresenting crime victims who were women or people of color (*Law and Order: SVU* had the second most women victims but the lowest number of victims of color), one of the most concerning trends in popular shows is the way they normalized or even justified behaviors that are harmful and illegal. These behaviors included questioning suspects without a lawyer, forcing confessions, excessive physical force, sexual harassment, corruption, failing to read Miranda rights, and racial profiling. The report found that of the 453 such actions depicted on police shows, only 3.7 percent (13 actions) included any accountability, and none of the accountability included firing or other serious consequences. Also, these actions were often not depicted as wrong. The report concludes, "One normalizing convention consistent across 18 of the 26 series examined was making wrongful actions seem right by depicting bad actions as being committed by 'Good Guy' characters, thereby framing wrongful actions as relatable, forgivable, acceptable and ultimately good." Since many of these wrongful actions were perpetrated by likable protagonists, these shows framed wrongful actions as "merely the cost of doing business when it comes to solving crimes, catching the bad guy and fighting for justice."[27] The report also notes that television shows about police have less racial and gender diversity in their producers and writers' rooms than other series.

Research shows modest but important impacts of shows like these on people's opinions of the police. A 2015 study led by political scientist Kathleen Donovan found that people who spent more than an hour a week watching police-themed TV dramas held the strongest positive opinions of the police and the strongest support for punitive responses to crime.[28] Consistent with other research, Donovan's team found discrepancies between fictional portrayals of law enforcement and reality, most notably that the majority of cases were serious crimes like murder, and the fictional officers almost always solved them. Just over two thousand people were surveyed about how much time per week they spent watching police dramas as well as follow-up questions about their opinions of police use of force. They were also asked about their demographic characteristics and political views as a way to assess whether the differences could be explained by people's preexisting beliefs rather than their viewing habits. Donovan's team found no significant differences in race, political beliefs, or whether they lived in urban, suburban, or rural areas. But there were significant differences between those who frequently watched police shows and those who did not. People who spent more than one hour per week watching police dramas were more likely to believe that the police were successful at reducing crime. They were also more likely than those who rarely or never watched crime dramas to believe that police misconduct does not lead to false confessions and that use of force by the police is necessary. Also, frequent viewers of crime drama were less likely to believe that the police use force excessively.

A 2024 study by Esteban Manuel Fernandez took this research design even further by randomly assigning people to watch either a ninety-second clip of *Chicago PD* or a reality show about home improvement. After watching the clips, participants were asked a series of questions about the police in their community including their feelings toward the police, their opinions on police reform issues like body cameras, and their opinions about whether the police are competent at preventing crimes and treating all ethnic groups equally. Among white people, those who watched ninety seconds of the police show were significantly more likely to express positive feelings toward the police. (Unexpectedly, this group also expressed more support for requiring the police to wear body cameras.) People of color who saw the crime drama clip reported more negative feelings toward the police.[29] Fernandez notes the limitations of a ninety-second clip compared to a typical television watcher who develops connections to fictional characters over an hour-long program or a multi-episode season, but the fact that he observed these changes in people who watched only ninety seconds of TV shows the power these dramas have.

Reading these dry but illuminating studies reminds me of my *Law and Order: SVU* phase. For years, I would come home from whatever attempt at stopping rape I'd made that day and sit in front of the TV watching three, even four episodes in a row. There was a fantasy I nurtured when I watched, a way I let myself believe that police departments dedicate armies of scientists to solving rapes. Rape kits on SVU came back from the lab in an hour. No fiber or hair follicle was left unanalyzed. Residue found under a victim's nails is linked to a Romanian trafficking ring or a ten-year-old cold case. But nothing sucked me in more than the squad room scenes, where the detectives sat behind steel-gray desks, drinking coffee out of cardboard Greek diner cups and shoehorned facts about rape into the dialogue.

The statute of limitations on a sex abuse case runs out five years after a victim's eighteenth birthday, Detective Olivia Benson would say. And

I didn't care how stiff the conversation sounded. I cheered the way sports fans do when their team scores a touchdown because I was that desperate for someone to give the TV viewing public accurate information about rape.

I loved the *SVU* detectives like the kind of friends you forgive no matter what, and there was nobody I loved as much as Olivia Benson. I wanted to be as driven and generous as she was. I wanted to be the kind of person a rape survivor could visit at three in the morning, the kind of person who would leave a first date to chase a suspect, climbing over fences in a dress and high heels. Even when my friends who worked at rape crisis centers criticized her for coercing survivors to testify in court, I forgave her. Even when she told a child that nobody would ever hurt her again, a promise no responsible person should make. I could justify ingesting high doses of pro-police fiction by telling myself that loving Olivia made me more of a feminist.

I wanted to make the solution to rape as simple as *SVU* did. Catch the bad guy. Put him away. Lather. Rinse. Repeat. And my love for the people and the emotional satisfaction of this most un-real and anti-real portrayal of what happens when a rape survivor goes to the police overpowered my reason because it soothed something deeper and more essential.

I was so emotionally invested in the characters that my love for them influenced my beliefs in ways I wasn't consciously aware of. I had developed a visceral disdain for defense lawyers that I didn't notice until a friend who worked as a defense lawyer pointed out that I always called prosecutors the "good guys." Even though my days working in courthouses were over, even though I worked with survivors whose experiences with real police officers were much more complicated than a formulaic TV show could contain, my heart was with Olivia and the rotating cast of detectives and district attorneys who could make rape investigations simple and satisfying.

The Law and Order franchise won my support by shutting off my mind. *SVU* tugged so hard at my heart, it gave me such a deep, visceral satisfaction that I was willing to agree with anything my flawed, fictional friends said. Without realizing that any of my beliefs had changed, I began seeing defense lawyers as obstructionists, as corrupt, as heartless impediments who stood between rape survivors and the justice they deserved. They enabled perpetrators ("perps" as Detective Elliot Stabler so often called them); they retraumatized brave and moral women and children who had already lived through sensational trauma. I believed all of these fictions without realizing I had formed beliefs.

Even when I thought my critical thinking was strong enough, my emotions won. They won by not competing. As a result, I was slower than I should have been to embrace restorative and transformative justice or community-safety workers that are building alternatives to the police. I was slower than I should have been to respect the essential role that defense lawyers play in holding the system accountable, especially when survivors of color are charged with crimes after they defend themselves.

This time around I won't be as unaware of the power of television fictions. I won't be as bewildered when architects of anxiety rage about crime. I will stay conscious of how much I crave the satisfaction of formulaic drama, and I will find it in places that won't manipulate my beliefs.

ACTION STEPS

For Yourself

- If you hear or read that crime is going up, dig deep into the sources before you get more worried. Zach Norris encourages us to understand and respect the complexity of why people's beliefs about crime may be so out of step with the evidence: "People's feeling of safety does not match with declining crime rates," he writes in *Defund Fear*. "Sometimes when confronted with this mismatch, researchers point to the role of the media and social media in sensationalizing and publicizing violent crimes. But this is only part of the answer. It's possible the research reflects people's fear of *harm* as opposed to crimes strictly defined—and their perception may be perfectly on point given rising inequality, patriarchy, and racism. Additionally, sometimes you don't *feel* safe even if all facts point to the reality of your *being* relatively safe, maybe because you've been hurt before and the trauma lingers and distorts reality, or because you are so encumbered by stress and anxiety that it skews your perception."[30]

- The Bureau of Justice Statistics publishes annual reports on National Crime Victimization Survey results that you don't need to be a criminologist to understand. While national trends might not be immediately useful to every person in every community, it could help you assess whether the news you consume is accurately reporting crime trends.
- If you love police shows, pay attention to how they may be shaping your opinions. If you're like me, it may be more than you realize.
- If you see someone posting a lot on social media about crime in your area, figure out who they are and who is funding them.

For Social Change

- If you have a truly local newspaper, ask hard questions about where they get their stories. Specifically, ask if law enforcement PR companies or public relations staff are feeding them stories and what they are doing to fact-check them. This can be emails to the editor or posts on your own social media when a law enforcement source is quoted and not fact-checked.
- Reach out to local crime reporters and push them to cover crimes like wage theft and pollution. There are great activists and advocacy groups that don't have the PR machines that police departments do. One example of a highly effective organization is Maintenance Cooperation Trust Fund (MCTF), available online at janitorialwatch.org. They organize non-union janitorial workers in California, a group that is primarily

Latina women, who are targeted for wage theft and sexual violence. Through a rare but effective collaboration with more ethical cleaning companies, MCTF leads campaigns to stop wage theft and sexual violence against janitorial workers. They have won back pay for workers from large corporations and advocated for legislative changes that increase protections. If your local media (or the folks on the Nextdoor app) are talking about crime, help them refocus on these far more consequential crimes.

- If the problem is that your local newspaper or TV station is under-resourced and that they are giving the police a megaphone solely because they have to fill more airtime than they have the staff to produce, collaborate with local activist and advocacy groups to produce press releases and videos that can be used. (Young people who are part of arts and activist organizations may be a great source for this; they can probably produce cool news segments with their phones.)
- Support criminal justice reformers, activists, leaders of violence prevention organizations, researchers, and others to get the attention of media and get themselves quoted in articles. If you have the time and energy, help these very busy and overtaxed activists develop relationships with reporters. If they are anything like me, they will appreciate the help.
- If you are feeling especially industrious, look at a year of reporting on crime in your local news outlets and see who they are quoting and what they are covering. Make that information known by reaching out to the editors, writing a letter to the editor, or posting on your own social media.
- Subscribe to nonprofit news sources like the Marshall Project that cover crime thoroughly and factually and are not beholden to corporate interests.

PART 3

WHAT YOU SHOULD NEVER DO

MYTH 6

"DON'T WEAR A PONYTAIL. AN ATTACKER COULD GRAB IT."

Don't wear a ponytail while you're on the street, especially at night. A ponytail gives an attacker something easy to grab so he can readily pull you away.[1] I found this directive on the now-defunct website selfdefenseforsmartwomen.com. Its owner, Harry Glick, is a retired prosecutor and accomplished martial artist. A man who I believe is sincere in his desire to help women stay safe. A few years ago, I got on Zoom with him and asked why he advises women to not wear ponytails. "It really depends on how old you are," he told me. "I have grandchildren with ponytails; I'm not going to tell them not to wear them!"

He gave me a long list of the bad things that can happen to people who wear ponytails. "A ponytail is something an assailant can easily grab onto," he told me. "That's the problem. An assailant can easily just grab onto it and pull you anywhere. So that's something I wouldn't recommend wearing. You can easily be strangled with a ponytail as well." After painting this scary but not factually substantiated picture, he abruptly changed the subject. "But to me, nowadays one of the worst things to wear are headphones; get rid of them," he said. "The most important thing you can do to protect yourself is to be aware and avoid potential danger. How can one be aware and avoid danger if they are focused on their music or whatever?"

"But your website does say ponytail," I pressed.

"It's just one of the so many things I can tell you—ponytails are one of them," he responded. But then he abruptly changed the subject again. Back to a familiar litany of reckless choices women make. "I saw this even today," he told me. "Women on their phones, they're talking while they're walking in the street, and they're listening to music, and have no clue what's going on around them. That's dangerous!"

Harry's website isn't the only source for ponytail panic. It's alive and well in an article that has a seemingly endless shelf life. Its title is "Through a Rapist's Eyes: Pls Take Time to Read This, It May Save a life, it may save your life." It's been around since at least the 1990s. Sometimes it's part of an email chain, other times it gets parked on websites and personal blogs. It's been published on local news sites in Michigan[2] and Louisiana,[3] and in the last decade, it has made its way to LinkedIn.[4]

With no author and no citations, it claims that "a group of rapists and date rapists in prison were interviewed on what they look for in a potential victim and here are some interesting facts." Chief among these alleged "facts" are the perils of the ponytail: "The first thing men look for in a potential victim is hairstyle. They are most likely to go after a woman with a ponytail, bun, braid, or other hairstyle that can easily be grabbed. They are also likely to go after a woman with long hair. Women with short hair are not common targets." This article also claims that rapists carry scissors and use them to cut apart our clothing. But fear not! Not everything we do is dangerous. All we have to do to deter these ponytail-obsessed, scissor-wielding rapists is carry an umbrella: "These men said they would not pick on women who have umbrellas, or other similar objects that can be used from a distance in their hands," the unnamed author claims. The object-cum-weapon needs to be big enough that rapists could see it from a distance, so clutching our keys in our fingers wouldn't work.

TikTok is breathing new life into ponytail warnings. And now they're being delivered by women. With titles like "Female Tip 101: Avoid wearing your hair in a ponytail when walking alone because it's easy to grab you by your ponytail,"[5] they give the same tired and unsubstantiated warnings. "If you tie your hair in a ponytail, it makes you an easy target," says Kasat Brown. "If someone is walking around and they're just a bad person, and they have to choose between a woman that has a ponytail and someone that doesn't, they would more likely go for the woman with the ponytail because it gives them something easy to grab onto. So that's what I think about before I go to the gym." Not planning her workout, not finding good music, but this intrusion of fear.

TikTok creator Brynn Baker posted a video called "Predator vs. Ponytail" that has thousands of likes and shares.[6] In it, she passes on the advice she got when she was in high school from her AP Environment teacher, a man she disliked. "He was basically explaining how predators, specifically male predators, prey on women who are alone, walking, and specifically wearing ponytails," she tells her followers. "A, the obvious: it's easy to grab onto, you can snatch her, whatever," she began. But then she gave a more involved explanation of what this teacher told his teenage students. "He started explaining how in men there's a primal instinct between prey and predator where a man turns into this primal animal and he goes after like a baby doe or a fawn because they have this tail, the white little tail that like swings back and forth so they know to prey on it."

"I don't know how true this is," she acknowledges, "he was like a crazy old man. But I think about it constantly, and if it can save somebody, then I hope it does." There is something sincere and urgent about her desire to help women. Jaded and sarcastic as I want to be, her video still breaks my heart every time I watch it. The story of man as predator and woman as prey is compelling and vivid. I imagine it resonates with women who have been overpowered and harmed by a man they thought they could trust. But at the same time, it was irresponsible for a science teacher to share this ridiculously sexist theory with his teenage students, many of whom were just starting to figure out dating, relationships, and intimacy.

No evidence connects hairstyle to higher rates of victimization. The National Crime Victimization Survey includes a 35-page,

174-question incident report. It asks detailed questions about everything from the location of the crime and the time of day to the demographic characteristics of everyone involved, but nothing about how anyone was wearing their hair.[7]

Telling women not to wear a ponytail is the ultimate example of the baseless safety advice that takes a mundane decision and casts it as an irresponsible risk. Rather than giving us reasonable explanations for why this precaution makes sense, the people who peddle this advice tell us fantastical stories about all the terrible things that could happen if we're dumb enough to tie up our hair.

Advice like this sets us up for failure: it's impossible to follow all the time, so we don't. If we're not careful, this can launch us into a vicious cycle. Not only are we afraid of being attacked, but now we also feel like we're being irresponsible. And then, if we are assaulted, especially on the street by a stranger, we feel like it's our fault. Ponytails are convenient. They keep long hair out of our faces, and they require less work than other hairstyles. If you want a few more minutes for your workout, your kids, your job, or your purpose in life, or if you just want to hit snooze one more time, all you have to do is spend a little less time on your hair. But if someone takes an authoritative tone and tells us that an inconsequential choice like tying back our hair puts us at risk for a crime as scary as abduction, it can launch us into a cycle of fear and self-censorship. Ponytail predator theories don't treat us like discerning, competent women. We are helpless fawns at the mercy of animalistic men and scissor-wielding rapists.

I know large-scale crime surveys have nothing to say about ponytail attacks, but I wanted to find out if there were even a few fact-checked accounts of women being seriously harmed by strangers who grabbed their ponytails. So I got on newspapers.com, a database that includes more than 11,000 publications dating back to 1900. News stories don't accurately represent how rare or common certain types of crimes are, but I wanted to find out if there was even one woman who experienced serious violence because someone grabbed her ponytail.

I found more references to ponytail attacks in articles that rehashed baseless safety advice than I did articles about hairstyle-involved crimes. And of the crime stories I found, none matched the warnings. In a 1991 article in the *Omaha World Herald*, a woman was putting her three-month-old baby into her car seat in a shopping center parking lot when a man came up behind her and cut off her ponytail.[8] When she yelled, the man ran away, leaving her and her baby unharmed. She reported the incident to the police, who chased the man but lost him. The article ends with a quote from the woman: "I'm getting it styled right away," she said about her newly short hair. It's worth noting that nobody in a crowded shopping center came to the woman's aid, and that her own powerful voice ended the attack. A similar ponytail crime made the *Minneapolis Star Tribune* in 1998.[9] A man who had cut a woman's ponytail on a busy street was sentenced to forty-five days in prison. Again, the woman was otherwise unharmed, and the man told reporters that he promised to get psychological help.

A 1989 article published in the *Spokane Chronicle* was a closer match to the crime pattern described in alarmist safety advice. Yet, the man who dragged a woman down a busy sidewalk by her ponytail was not a stranger, but her abusive ex-boyfriend.[10] The article noted that many people witnessed the attack, but no one intervened. A 2006 article in the *Daily Telegraph* in London included a similar story of an abusive boyfriend cutting off a woman's ponytail.[11]

The article I found that most closely matched the elaborate stories included in the baseless warnings about the perils of ponytails is about a woman who was tragically killed, not by a human "predator" but by a shark. In 2010, at SeaWorld in Florida, a shark grabbed trainer Dawn Brancheau by her ponytail and dragged her underwater, holding her by her hair until she drowned.[12]

When I imagine a ponytail grab, I see a range of possibilities. This is what I love about feminist self-defense, or any form of self-defense training that helps people build their problem-solving skills. Not "how vividly can I describe an assault so that I scare myself and others?" but "what can I do to stop this assault?" My first option would be to make noise—the woman in Omaha in 1991 scared the ponytail cutter with her loud voice. But if a loud voice doesn't stop the threat, there are physical skills I can use. If I'm trying to figure out how to get out of a ponytail grab or any other tight spot, I ask two questions: *What's free on me? What's vulnerable on the person who is trying to hurt me?* My answers to these questions inform my resistance strategy.

First, the hand that is grabbing my ponytail can't do anything else. Yes, hair pulling can hurt, but it doesn't obstruct my breathing or tie up the rest of my body. Also, a person who grabs my ponytail is putting himself in the perfect position to be hit in the face. If I forcefully strike him with my elbow (or the little area above my elbow that forms the base of my triceps muscle), I can cause enough pain to end the threat even if the ponytail attacker is bigger and more muscular than me. This is what IMPACT Boston teaches. For a physical skill, I want to use a strong part of my body against a weak part of his. His eyes, head, and face are vulnerable. Eyes can't function with even a speck of dust in them, much less a hard elbow bone. A nose can break or bleed, a strike to the throat can interrupt his breathing for a few seconds. So if I can reach the face, I can probably end the attack, or at the very least, make it hard for him to keep hold of the ponytail. If he's quick enough to block his face, and strong enough to do that without losing his grip on my ponytail, then he leaves the rest of his body unprotected. In that case, I can slap his groin or stomp on his foot. There is no self-defense strategy that works in every situation, but the more options I can find, the more clearly I see that I don't have to restrict my life.

ACTION STEPS

For Yourself

- Think critically when you are told that a mundane activity is dangerous. Especially if the person giving the advice doesn't offer any evidence.
- Reframe your mindset. There are weak parts of everyone's body, even the biggest, most muscular, most athletic man you can imagine. If you use a physical skill, it's probably most effective to strike a part of the body that is impossible to strengthen like the eyes, head, groin, or throat. Choose self-defense techniques that involve simple movements with your body. (That cool-looking spinning kick you saw in an action movie is probably not something you're going to remember when you're under stress!)
- Also, learn some physical skills that could end the threat against you even if they are not executed perfectly (most of us are going to be nervous!). Using our fingers to strike the eyes or the palm of our hand against the nose are good examples of this. Even if you miss the target, you're likely to cause a flinch reaction that could buy you time to either get away or do another strike. And if the person responds by grabbing your arms, then their arms are occupied too. They can't simultaneously hold your arms and block both their head and their groin, so you could have a cleaner target to hit the groin. The goal is not to look cool or be an Ultimate Fighting Champion; it's to compromise their ability to hurt you. There's no perfect kick or strike, just two useful questions: What's free on me? What's vulnerable on the person who is trying to hurt me?
- Think of the women in the news stories in this chapter and others, and remember the power of a forceful voice. If I have a choice between verbal and physical self-defense techniques, I'm always going to choose my voice. If someone doesn't touch

me (or if they only touch my hair) and I don't touch them, my chances of getting injured are a lot lower.
- Wear a ponytail if you want. Don't worry about it.

For Social Change

- If you're good at social media, create your own content. People who spread baseless safety advice are not the only ones who can post engaging videos!
- If your local police department or university posts the "Through a Rapist's Eyes" article (or if a colleague posts it in LinkedIn), ask hard questions. Push them to cite their sources and give you a good answer for why they chose it. If you can't get an answer from them, post something on your own social media. Pay special attention to taxpayer-funded city or county departments that spread baseless safety advice and call attention to them in public or at town or city council meetings.

MYTH 7

"DON'T PARK NEXT TO A VAN (ESPECIALLY WHITE VANS OR VANS WITH TINTED WINDOWS)"

In a video called "5 Things I Don't Do as a Woman Running Errands Alone," TikTok influencer Cassidy Milan brings new life to the tired advice that tells women not to park near a van. She talks about a time she was followed around a supermarket by a man who was coming up behind her and grunting.[1] She ran out of the store, got into her car, and drove away. But instead of acknowledging that she saved herself, she expresses regret that she didn't try to get help from the police officer who was in the store. "Looking back," she says, "I 100% would have gone to the police officer and let him know what happened, and have him walk me to my car and file a report." Women can and do rescue ourselves, but too often we second-guess that decision.

In the video, she is poised and certain. The van advice comes at the end of a predictable list—she never leaves her car door unlocked while pumping gas, she never sits in her car outside a store or restaurant. She even goes so far as to advise women not to take the time to put a destination into their GPS because that would involve sitting in their car in a parking lot. She then describes her elaborate routine for loading groceries into her car without turning her back to the parking lot. She puts her butt on her trunk and twists around to load each grocery bag because if she turned her back to the parking lot, then an attacker could grab her from behind and throw her into a van. "It is so easy for them to slide open that back door and just throw you in there," she explains.

If baseless safety advice had a Top 40 song that was played so incessantly that its grating-but-catchy melody was perpetually stuck in our heads, it would be this one: Don't park near a van. Or a white van. Or a van with tinted windows. There's a hundred other van warning videos on social media: the one with ominous music and stock photos of white vans along with cautionary messages about how sliding doors make it easy to grab you.[2] There's the one where Christmas music plays while silent, stern-faced TikTok influencer Michael Genay points to directives that appear over his head on the screen. The directives tell women not to park near vans while shopping for the holidays because men in vans are waiting in parking lots to accost us.[3] I reached out to him through his website to ask where he got the information about van crime, and perhaps unsurprisingly, I did not get an answer.

But this advice predates TikTok by decades. Sometimes it's straightforward, like the Rape Aggression Defense (RAD) manual, which tells women to "try to avoid parking next to vans or trucks and be cautious when returning to a vehicle parked near a van or large truck."[4] Or Women Against Crime telling women and teen girls: "If you notice someone suspicious or a van parked next to your car, return to the store and ask for help rather than approaching your vehicle alone."[5]

Other times it's more elaborate, full of dramatic stories about bad people who jump out of vans and the labor-intensive steps that women should take to avoid becoming their victims. The Sun Lakes Sherriff's department directs women: "If you return to your vehicle to find a van parked next to your driver's side door, either enter through the passenger side and lock your doors behind you, or return to the store and ask for an escort to your car. Predators sometimes use vans next to vehicles to aide [*sic*] in abductions in parking lots."[6] But, as the Desoto County Sheriff's department in Florida warns, we shouldn't get just any security officer to escort us. "Do not go up to just any security guard. Go directly to the kiosk and ask for them to assign an officer to escort you. Predators sometimes dress up to resemble security or other authority figures."[7]

I went looking through federal crime data, and the most recent reports on actual violent crimes show that only 6 percent take place in parking lots, compared to the almost 50 percent of crimes that are committed in households. To be fair, the FBI documented increased reports of car thefts between 2019 and 2023, but nothing like the scenarios described in safety tips. I also asked the Bureau of Justice Statistics if they had any data that support or debunk this advice. I got an email from a scientist explaining that in the NCVS results, they created a combined category of "commercial place, parking lot, other public area" because otherwise there would not be enough incidents to do proper statistical analysis.

In the absence of large-scale data, I put the words "woman," "van," and "abduction" (plus a few variations) into Google to see how news stories about actual crimes diverged from the well-worn advice. I'm not suggesting that local news, or local news that is optimized for Google, is any kind of representative sample of violence. But since research shows local news overrepresents stranger violence and violent crime compared to property crime, I wanted to see how many parking-lot van abductions I could find even in this skewed sample.

I spent hours I will never get back reviewing the first hundred local news stories that came up in response to my searches. Not surprisingly, there was not one that matched the horrendous warnings. Also, even when using "woman" in the search, the majority of stories I found were about children, not adult women, being approached by people in vans. Of the hundred stories I reviewed, forty-one were about adults and the remaining fifty-nine were about teenagers or children. Of the stories about women being dragged into vans, twenty-one involved boyfriends, exes, or other people they knew, compared to only fourteen by strangers. (There were six stories where the relationship was unknown or not reported by the newscast, and one of those stories was about a man.)

In one story, a woman in Arizona was at a rest stop where she handed a Post-it Note to another customer.[8] The note directed the customer to call 911 and gave useful information about the make of the car and its license plate. The police eventually found the van and arrested the man who had taken her. It was someone she knew. Her mother had called the police to report her daughter missing and given the driver's name as the person who likely abducted her. In a similar story in Las Vegas, a neighbor tried to help a woman who was dragged from her apartment by a man believed to be an ex-boyfriend. The neighbor got the license plate, and the woman was found in New Mexico.[9] Some of the stories were heartbreaking. In one story in Los Angeles County, a man was using a van to serially rape women. The women and teen girls he targeted were undocumented, so they didn't report to police.[10] Of the adult women in the news stories I found, there were some tragic outcomes—three were found dead, two seriously injured, and three were still missing. But in the majority, twenty-five out of forty-one were safe (in the remaining eight stories, the outcome was not reported or not known at the time the story aired).

Most of the stories I found about van crime were about kids who were approached by an adult they didn't know who tried to get them into a van, but in forty-one of the stories, the kids got away. In an additional seven, kids were rescued by the police or other adults. So 81 percent got away completely unharmed. The stories were so similar that I had to check myself several times to make sure they weren't duplicates.

A boy in Riverton, Utah, was approached by adults who tried to get him into their car by luring him with candy. He ran away, tried to get into his own house, but found the door locked. When the car didn't leave, he picked up rocks from his front walk and prepared to throw them at the car.[11] Another boy in Leesburg, Georgia, was offered cookies, but since his mom had talked to him about stranger danger, he knew to run away.[12] A nine-year-old girl in Sanger, California, was walking home from school when a man grabbed her and put her into a van.[13] She screamed so loud that the attackers let her out. In another story, an eleven-year-old girl was attacked by a man with a knife at a bus stop who tried to get her into his van. She was playing with slime, and she rubbed it in his face and ran away.

Local news stories about dangerous people in vans follow a consistent pattern: child gets approached or lured by a stranger, child understands immediately that the situation is not safe, child runs away, makes noise, throws rocks, puts toy slime in the attacker's face. The resistance of an eight- or nine- or eleven-year-old kid overwhelms the attacker, so the attacker gives up and takes off while the kid gets to safety. The parents then talk about how scared they were and, in some cases, how upsetting it is to know that something like this can happen in their quiet suburban neighborhood, and then the police (or school officials if the incident happened while the kid was walking home from school) urge caution, without clearly defining what that caution might look like.

What could the world look like if children felt entitled to resist that powerfully if the person trying to hurt them was someone they knew? What if they knew they'd be believed, and not just believed but praised for being strong and sticking up for themselves?

Child sexual abuse, which is much more common than abduction, is almost never done by a stranger. According to the CDC, 91 percent of child sexual abuse is from someone the child or parents know and trust. But even the majority of abductions are committed by familiar people. Criminologist Jeffrey Walsh led a study that analyzed 29,293 child abduction cases that had been reported to law enforcement through the National Incident-Based Reporting System (NIBRS) between 1995 and 2013.[14] Walsh's team identified four categories of victim/offender relationship: family, acquaintance, stranger, and intimate partner. They found that the majority of abductions were from someone the child knew: 48.2 percent were family members, often a noncustodial or estranged parent. The next highest category was acquaintances at 26.8 percent. Dating partners made up 9.3 percent. So added together, familiar people made up 84.3 percent of abductions. Only 15.6 percent of abductions reported to NIBRS-participating law enforcement agencies were by strangers.

Also, in contrast to the majority of news stories I identified, Walsh found that in two-thirds of abductions, children were taken from their homes, not the park or the mall or the other public places a lot of us reflexively fear. They also found that the majority of these abductions did not involve weapons and that in the majority of cases, children were not seriously injured.

Still, when you ask kids—or even adults—about safety, it won't be long before you hear the phrase "stranger danger." "Stranger Danger" educational campaigns entered the public consciousness in the late 1970s and early '80s, when a small number of high-profile abductions of white boys made national news. Historian Paul Renfro traced the prominence of this concept to the 1981 abduction of Adam Walsh from a department store in Florida.[15] His parents, John and Revé, rose to national prominence through TV appearances. John Walsh went on to become the host of the long-running TV series *America's Most Wanted* and was a key player in the political activism that led to increased national attention and resources invested in stopping stranger abductions. This included missing children's pictures on milk cartons and television PSAs asking parents the ominous question "Do you know where your children are?"

The Walshes and other parents of white children who had faced horrific but rare violence advocated for some of the harshest punishments of those who harm children. And they did so with exaggerated statistics. The Walshes and others publicly stated that fifty thousand children were abducted by strangers every year, though actual evidence put the number somewhere between one hundred and three hundred. And despite the lack of evidence that Adam had experienced sexual abuse,[16] a 2006 law that required all US states to maintain publicly available registries of people convicted of sex crimes was named for him.[17] Sex offender registration laws remain popular across the political spectrum despite the lack of evidence that they have any effect on recidivism.[18]

Renfro documents the impact of these parents' visibility on public opinion throughout the 1980s and '90s, including a 1987 poll by the public option research firm Roper, which found that 76 percent of children were "very concerned" about being kidnapped. Kidnapping was the most common fear in that poll, more common

Renfro notes, than nuclear war or AIDS.[19] That same year, a study of Midwestern fifth graders found that half of them ranked someone grabbing them as their biggest concern and 44 percent said it was "likely or highly likely" that they would become missing children. A 1991 Mayo Clinic survey of parents found that 72 percent said they feared their children might be abducted, and one-third named kidnapping as a "frequent worry." This study found that kidnapping was rated higher than any other concern, including car accidents.[20]

Renfro argues that this stranger danger panic was a conservative reaction to social and political progress and sexual liberation movements, and the focus on white boys abducted by men fueled homophobia that was intensifying in the wake of the AIDS epidemic. A small number of white boys who were abducted by strangers were all over the media. "The imagery of endangered childhood also reified the idea that young Americans—specifically the photogenic, middle-class, white bodies to whom childhood innocence is so readily assigned—faced new or intensifying threats from deviant strangers emboldened by sexual liberation."[21] Renfro goes on to describe the political impact of this "endangered childhood" frame: "the child protection campaign and its attendant logic of sexualized stranger danger became virtually unassailable in the early eighties. Few dared to challenge the movement or the faulty statistics animating it."[22]

Sympathy for bereaved white parents of children who had been victims of horrific crimes existed across the political spectrum, from liberal senators like Paul Simon to conservative then president Ronald Reagan. This created political will for law-and-order policies and was one of the many factors that fueled mass incarceration. Renfro argues that constitutional victories achieved by criminal defendants in having rights and due process created panic, and the moral authority of bereaved parents was an effective way to turn public opinion against these reforms. Scary strangers snatching kids from Midwestern baseball fields generated more public sympathy and urgency than structural threats to children's safety and well-being like poverty, hunger, and underfunded schools.

Renfro contrasts the public outrage over white boys to a much larger number of poor and working-class Black children who were abducted and murdered in Atlanta between 1979 and 1981.[23] Not only did their cases not receive nearly as much media attention, but working-class Black children were not portrayed by the media as being "innocent" the way white children were. Some of the children were poor and ran errands for others to earn money. Because of this, news reporters characterized them as "street hustlers." And while the innocence of eleven-year-old white paper boys in Iowa (which is arguably the white suburban equivalent of running errands to earn money) who were abducted was a major focus of the media coverage, eleven-year-old Black children in Atlanta were not afforded that same innocence. "The *Atlanta Journal-Constitution*, for one, claimed that eleven-year-old victim Patrick Baltazar was '[a]ll grown up' and 'leading a man's life.' The youngster had 'learned to make his own way in the world of adults.' For his part, a local public safety official even called Baltazar 'a hustler from the word go.'"[24] Even without physical evidence, news media described the slain boys as "known to travel with adult homosexuals" and exchange sex for money.[25] A poll of Black parents in Atlanta in 1981 found that 79 percent believed that the killings would have gotten more media attention if the children were white.

While experts and child safety advocates have moved away from telling children that all strangers are dangerous (noting that kids in trouble might be reluctant to get help from a store clerk or police officer if they believe they should distrust all strangers), the message that violence comes from outsiders is still pervasive.

Still, what I get from these stories is more complicated. I look at them and see the agency and power of children. When children are told that a type of situation is dangerous and when they trust that adults will praise them for resisting, they do. And when they do, for the most part, they get free. When they are given the information and permission to trust their internal sense of danger, they can do a lot to protect themselves. The kids in the news made noise, ran away, threw rocks. They knew it was OK to hurt an adult to keep that adult from hurting them.

Even with the handful of parents who told local news reporters how upset they were to discover a creepy adult lurking in their quiet suburban community, acknowledging that a stranger was trying to hurt their kid doesn't disrupt very much. None of them had to struggle with their decisions about who they trusted. They didn't have to agonize about whether to give up a sport or a religious community they loved; they didn't have to leave home or kick a family member out. They didn't have to give up dependable childcare or face the hot rage of other people's denial. A candy-wielding stranger in a van can be branded as a "bad person" without disrupting power structures in families or institutions.

It is possible to teach kids the skills to resist unsafe attention without pretending that strangers are the only threat. It's not as prevalent as "stranger danger" warnings, nor is it well researched. But parents I interviewed gave me hope that giving children clear, specific, and empowering information is possible. Growing up, Laurie Gordon (a pseudonym) got a lot of unwanted attention from adults and older kids she knew. But the only people her parents warned her about were strangers. She grew up in the 1980s. Her family was one of thousands that saw missing kids on their milk cartons and heard stern warnings about child molesters on TV. So when she was harmed by people she knew as a teenager and young adult, she was unprepared. "I was aware of not feeling protected in any way, and having to be on my own," she tells me.

When Laurie became a parent, she wanted her daughter to have better information and more support. From the time her daughter was little, Laurie told her that if anyone in their family made her uncomfortable, it was always OK to ask for help. When she didn't feel comfortable spending time with a relative, Laurie always agreed to go with her so they wouldn't be alone together. She doesn't believe this relative was abusive, but he held some sexist beliefs and shared them with Laurie's daughter in ways she didn't like. Watching her daughter repeatedly ask for and get support in uncomfortable situations has been a joy. Now that her daughter is a teenager, she loves watching how easy it is for her to set boundaries with this relative. "She's actually better at dealing with him now than I am because I still feel that Mama Bear rage," Laurie tells me. Her daughter, by contrast, is "so good at turning everything into humor and deflecting it right back at him."

Laurie loves watching her daughter with her friend group, noticing how much she has internalized the message that it's OK to have boundaries with people you know, that it's OK to get help if someone you're supposed to trust makes you uncomfortable. That said, it's not easy for any of us, especially a teenager, to do this all the time. "She talks to her friends about how important it is to take care of yourself," she tells me. "But she doesn't always practice what she preaches. That is a struggle. I don't know who does. But I can see how good a friend she is to other kids. She really helps to teach people how worthy of self-respect that they are. I think the ecosystem of teenagers is stronger as a result of her learning to care for her own needs."

Tashmica Torok was the founding executive director of the Firecracker Foundation, a healing and advocacy organization for children and teens that have survived sexual abuse. What sticks with her from her years of finding creative ways to support and advocate for kids of all ages is the betrayal they experience when they are abused by someone they know. It's not just betrayal but utter disorientation, especially when they've been told their whole lives that "family is everything" and "blood is thicker than water." Tashmica believes that not preparing kids for the possibility that they could be harmed by someone they know creates more vulnerability. So does growing up in a family where adults tolerate or ignore abusive or inappropriate behavior from other adults.

Not wanting to lie to her own kids, and also not wanting to scare them, Tashmica has been creative and nuanced in how she parents. When they began having sleepovers at their cousins' and friends' homes, Tashmica gave them helpful, concrete information. "I was always checking in about 'So where did you sleep? What was the situation, which room were you guys in, which kids were there, what adults were there?' And trying to just be casual: 'Tell me about the party. What happened? What did you watch? What did you do?' And always reminding them that at no time should anybody be trying to sleep in their sleeping bag, like, be bothering them at night. 'Nighttime is for sleep time. So if someone is waking you up, you can call me. I'll come and get you. Like, this is not a normal thing that happens with sleepovers.'" This is a great example of helping kids understand what's inappropriate without scaring or overwhelming them. Her kids are teenagers now, and she's separated from their father and starting to date. The messages about safety and boundaries are more sophisticated now. She makes sure they know that she will always choose them if someone she dates makes them feel uncomfortable or unsafe. They roll their eyes when she says it, but she doesn't care. It's important to her to keep having the fortitude for uncomfortable truths.

There are a million creative ways to tell kids the truth without scaring them. Tashmica's concrete example of what's supposed to happen at a sleepover is a perfect illustration of how adults can frame the conversation. Parents give young children information about how the world works all the time: *this is how you tie your shoes; this is how you act in a restaurant; this is what happens at the doctor's office, and this is why it's OK to take your clothes off here but not at the dentist.* Parents could seamlessly include information about attention that isn't appropriate from adults they know: *when you're at gymnastics class, all the kids should be together in the gym.* Just as important is Laurie's practice of being available to help her daughter navigate other adults. Being trustworthy and present and helpful emboldens kids to honor their boundaries.

I will never forget the news story about the girl who fought off a man who tried to grab her with slime. She is as brave and creative and resourceful as all children can be when adults have the skills and courage to back them up.

ACTION STEPS

For Yourself

- Park next to a van. Don't worry about it. If you live in a crowded city, you're probably lucky to find legal parking anywhere.
- If you are a parent, teach your kid that they can choose who they touch. And back them up when other adults try to touch them in ways they don't like. Teaching kids that they get to decide who they hug or kiss helps them learn their boundaries. Showing them you respect their boundaries, and you will support them when other adults might not, can help them learn to expect not to be touched in ways they don't like. This makes it easier for your kid to recognize boundary violations that are subtle and covert and to resist unwanted sexual advances across the lifespan.

For Social Change

- If people in your community are upset by an incident involving a stranger, remind them of the statistical realities and engage them in prevention efforts that include focusing on familiar people.
- If you are part of social media groups of parents who circulate warnings about stigmatized strangers, respond with factual information about the majority of sexual abuse and abduction.

MYTH 8

"MAKE SURE PEOPLE CAN'T SEE THROUGH YOUR WINDOWS, ESPECIALLY WHEN YOU'RE UNDRESSED"

The Rape Aggression Defense (RAD) manual, among other directives, includes this piece of advice: "Draw the drapes and pull the shades. If the drapes are thin or worn, you may want to consider investing in heavier fabric to prevent silhouetting."[1]

I first encountered this directive when I participated in a RAD instructor training in 2008. The man who led the training presented it in the form of a story: A fellow police officer was casing his house to see if he could experience it the way a criminal would. His wife was upstairs changing clothes in the bedroom, and he could see her naked through the window. So the man in the story talked to his wife, telling her that if he could see her changing, bad people could, and she should be more careful.

I raised my hand and asked the question that would become my personal brand: *Is there evidence that any large number of crimes start with perpetrators seeing their victims undress through the windows?* The police officer leading the training responded by saying *we don't have time to get into all that.* That wasn't the first time I'd been dismissed or deflected when I challenged someone, but that moment stuck with me more than the others. Maybe because this wasn't a lecture for the public; it was a training program for people who were going to be teaching self-defense. It surprised me, maybe more than it should have, that the officer leading the training didn't seem to think it was important to make sure teachers understood the reasoning behind what we told our students.

If I were a superhero or a supervillain, that moment would be my origin story. It was the moment I realized that critical thinking was not welcome (by the end of the three-day training course, everyone was making fun of me for asking too many questions). It was the moment I saw with a new clarity how a man could communicate certainty and authority but not feel any responsibility to provide evidence. That question, like most of my questions, was treated like an annoying mosquito that snuck in through a hole in the screen door.

Years later, I reached out to the Bureau of Justice Statistics to ask if there was any data to support the idea that crimes are committed by men who spy women through uncurtained windows. "BJS does not have data that could answer this question," they responded. There's something particularly frustrating about advice like this. It can't be proven or disproven. Unlike the "victim walk," there's no cluster of studies that give nuance to overstated claims. Unlike claims that crime is on the rise, there are no reams of data to demonstrate that it's false.

So when I see safety advice like this, advice that can't be corroborated or debunked, I ask a different question: *What are the values or assumptions that underlie this advice?* In other words, *what is the agenda of the advice?* And, more importantly, *do I agree with it?* As a teacher, I give a lot of suggestions that don't have an evidence base because they've never been studied. There isn't any published research on strategies for de-escalating conflicts at protests or ways of holding boundaries with immigration enforcement officers who are trying to get into domestic violence shelters without a warrant. But I believe in the strategies I teach and the values that underlie them. I believe, too, that the need for safety strategies in these situations and a number of others is compelling enough to use my best judgment in the absence of relevant research.

If we apply those questions to the RAD advice, the underlying values are that modesty is safety. Women's bodies being on display, intentionally or not, is treated as a risk for violence. Not unlike the litany of directives we get about not wearing short skirts, it's another statement that women who don't cover ourselves enough—even in our own homes!—are somehow more rape-able, or at the very least, more at fault if we are raped.

To be clear, if you value modesty, having thick curtains or keeping them closed may make sense for you. Also, we live in a world where we are photographed and surveilled without our knowledge or consent, so that may be a consideration for you. But if modesty is not your concern, and you're instead looking for practical ways to reduce your risk for violence, then buying thicker drapes might not make the most sense.

ACTION STEPS

For Yourself

- When you get safety advice that can't be confirmed or debunked, think about the values or the agenda behind it. Your decision about whether to take the advice may be based on whether you agree with the agenda.

For Social Change

- It can be important to challenge any message that equates modesty with safety, specifically if it's directed at young women. Think critically about advice like this, and whether it's just a different way of telling women to "cover up" or "not distract men."

MYTH 9

"DON'T GO SHOPPING ALONE. OTHERWISE YOU COULD BE A TARGET OF HUMAN TRAFFICKERS."

In a blog post on the website of Women Against Crime, an organization founded by retired police officer and stalking survivor Trish Hoffman, women are directed not to go shopping alone (or be spaced out and distracted while they do their errands) because if they do, the human traffickers might get them.[1] "If someone seems to be following you or paying you too much attention, take note and be ready to take action," Hoffman advises. "This is particularly important given the alarming rise in human trafficking, where traffickers often prey on those who appear distracted or vulnerable." The site also urges shoppers that "retail environments, including grocery stores, can unfortunately serve as a hunting ground for traffickers. They exploit these public spaces to observe and target potential victims, using tactics like grooming and manipulation to lure them."

"Younger girls are often more vulnerable to stalking and human trafficking," Hoffman says, "because they may be less experienced in recognizing dangerous situations and are more likely to be trusting, making them easier targets for predators." If you click on the links embedded in these alarming statements, they will take you to news stories that are not about trafficking. One is about a man in Chicago who tried unsuccessfully to abduct a nine-year-old girl from a store, the other features a woman who reported a "suspicious" man to the police.

Warnings like this are all over social media. TikTok creator Big Nic's video "Ladies if you see a van that looks suspicious don't park by it" is full of elaborate scenarios of women being stalked by human traffickers who hide out in vans in Walmart parking lots.[2] Using the hashtag #humantraffickingawareness, Molllyydoll claims that she was almost trafficked.[3] What actually happened is that she was at Walmart getting milk at 9 p.m., and when she left the store, a man was walking behind her. She describes him as a "short-statured man in all black, black hat, black hoodie, textbook definition." She turned around and yelled, at which point the man in the dark hoodie ran away and got into the passenger side of a car that was running. The car drove away. Then, a passenger in a nearby construction van shut his door and drove away. KatyIronman has a similar video in which she concludes that she was almost trafficked because she was sitting in her car in a parking lot at a mall, looking at her phone, when a van with tinted windows pulled into a spot next to hers. The man in the van then reclined his seat all the way back.[4] She doesn't get through the five-plus-minute video without criticizing herself for being distracted by her phone and thanking god for protecting her.

One difference between human trafficking and other baseless safety advice is that the most outrageous claims are routinely debunked. A local news station in Elizabethtown, Kentucky, ran a story that urged people not to believe Facebook posts claiming that traffickers put the letter "X" on the cars they were planning to target.[5] A TV news station in Midland, Texas, quotes a police department representative reassuring the public that a viral Facebook post about traffickers in a Walmart parking lot was false.[6] The *Newport Daily News* ran a story in which the police and a Walmart store manager debunked a Facebook post claiming that young women were prohibited from applying for jobs because traffickers were hiding in the store's parking lot, waiting to lure them to the Motel 6 across the street.[7]

This pattern has been going on for more than a decade—someone gets on social media to describe a person in a parking lot who scared them, sometimes with reasonably scary actions, other times just for wearing dark clothing or driving a beat-up van. Then, the police reassure the public that they are not at risk. As far back as 2015, the fact-checking website Snopes was debunking claims about trafficking, like one posted on Facebook about a man with a white van who was supposedly pressuring women to take makeup samples, and if they complied, he would throw them into his van.[8]

But even when the hyperbolic social media post is met with the calm, steady reassurance of a police spokesperson, the most important realities about human trafficking get lost. Jean Bruggeman is the executive director of Freedom Network USA, a Washington, DC–based organization that works to prevent trafficking and support survivors. Jean, I imagine, is more tired of hearing about traffickers hiding in Walmart parking lots than I am of hearing about the perils of putting your hair up. Freedom Network USA was founded in 2001 by legal advocates and service providers who were working on some of the largest labor and sex trafficking cases at the time. These were cases about actual trafficking—impoverished people, often undocumented immigrants, who were forced to work for low or no pay in buildings that were not up to code. In one case, workers were locked inside factories.

What advocacy groups like Freedom Network USA want us to understand about trafficking, Jean tells me, is that "these forms of forced labor did have elements of threats of violence or violence, but what was really keeping people stuck in that situation were not those threats. It was the coercion, and it involved manipulation of the legal system, of cultural beliefs and of language access." Real and factual understandings of trafficking point to systemic change as the way to end it. "The way to really end this crime is to ensure people's human rights," she says. "So if traffickers are manipulating our immigration system in order to threaten and to abuse immigrants, then what we need to change is the immigration system, not the immigrants."

Trafficking, Jean reminds me, is an exploitation of people's labor. And while the types of trafficking that involve forced sex work get lodged in our most prurient, sensational imaginations, many more trafficking victims are harvesting our food and making our clothes. And people are vulnerable to traffickers not because they were insufficiently aware of their surroundings when they stopped at Walmart, but because they are systematically denied their rights. "Traffickers are enabled whenever governments are willing to compromise people's human rights," Jean explains. "When we do not allow them freedom of movement, then a trafficker takes advantage of that. So where we limit immigrants as to where they can work, when they can move, how they can move, which borders they can cross, then we're inviting traffickers to take advantage of that." And it's not just immigrants. "When we refuse to allow trans kids to show up as their whole selves in our schools," she explains, "what we're doing is inviting traffickers to take advantage of them. When we refuse to make housing affordable, then we put poor people into the crosshairs of traffickers."

Trafficking targets the most vulnerable workers. "We all have friends who have taken a terrible job where the manager is outrageous, the pay is not what it was promised to be," Jean explains. If a person with privilege is in that situation, we can resign. But, Jean tells me, "a human trafficking victim can't, because there would be some kind of harm that would occur to their family members, to themselves, or the trafficker has created a situation in which they are physically isolated, they're isolated by language, and so they cannot get away. With folks who are not English language speakers, if you're in a rural town in Georgia, working on a farm, how are you going to ask for help if all you speak is Thai?" So traffickers recruit workers who are vulnerable. Even some workers who are in the US legally can be targeted. "We see a lot of trafficking of workers with H-1 visas, temporary worker visas," Jean says, "because the visa does not allow them to just say, 'I don't like this employer. I'm going to find a different one.' It's not that easy. And so the employer says you have two choices: you can stay here and take it, or you can go back. And you probably had to pay a recruiter in the home country to connect you to that job, that great opportunity in America where everything is gold and milk and honey, and so you owe debt back home that you can never repay. Those are the circumstances that are created, which is why workers don't need to be locked in, they don't need to be tied down, they don't need to be physically entrapped, because there's so many other systemic factors that entrap them."

Another group that is trafficked is youth who are kicked out of their homes, often for being LGBTQ+, or youth who leave home to escape abuse. But these realities don't match the stories we want to tell ourselves. As a country, Jean says, "we love a rescue narrative. We want to swoop in to a poor, sad victim who's been abused and exploited," she says. "Frankly, the more abuse, the better. We feel much more sorry for a person who has visible injuries, who has been exploited in very visible ways, and is willing to talk about it in graphic detail. For those folks, we want to help them." But while we in the US yearn for a sympathetic, redeemable victim, Jean says, "what has made all forms of abuse and exploitation so intractable in this country is our refusal to address the root causes."

"Why do people feel trapped in an exploitive job? Because there is no safe place for them to go, because our legal system makes it very complicated." Sometimes, trafficking victims have debt in their home countries that they can't pay, other times they have criminal records because the labor they've been forced to do is illegal, which can make them ineligible for public housing and other services. There are systematic policy choices, Jean says, that keep people stuck.

"It's labor recruiters who are falsifying documents or lying about the conditions," Jean explains, "or bringing you to an isolated place to do work where you're stuck because there's no public transportation for you to leave. It's people engaged in grooming young people into sex work by promising them a better life than the life that they're struggling with."

Labor trafficking is more common than sex trafficking. It's prevalent in industries that require a lot of human labor, like meat and seafood processing or harvesting crops that aren't mechanized. Jean points me to a National Institute of Justice study that found that a quarter of agricultural workers in North Carolina experienced some form of labor abuse, and 18 percent experienced incidents that meet the legal definition of trafficking. This was true despite the fact that only 17 percent of the workers were undocumented.[9] And despite the Facebook posts and TikTok videos, the reality is that the trafficker is an entire system, not a guy in a dark hoodie or a man reclining in the passenger seat of his beat-up van. A man who is probably just trying to get a little sleep between his night job and his day job.

There are corporate structures that separate us, the buyers of vegetables and fruit and meat, from the people who produce them. Small farms, Jean tells me, are the exception, but with large agribusiness, there is one company that owns the land. A different company oversees the farming, and a different company oversees the pickers. That company hires another company that hires a crew boss to supervise the workers. In the United States, an employer is responsible for the working conditions of the people on their payroll, but if they hire a contractor, they don't have any obligation to make sure that company's employees are safe. So, Jean tells me, if the farm has no bathrooms for workers or pays less than minimum wage or not at all, and the workers are employees of a contractor of a contractor of a contractor, then none of the labor violations are legally the landowner's problem.

"The system is designed to insulate the people with the real money," she says. "You've got crew bosses who are rounding up workers, transporting them from farm to farm to do work. They're certainly exploiting these workers, but they're not rich." When it comes to illegal and unsafe working conditions, she explains, "the crew boss is certainly the most responsible, so, if you're looking for criminal responsibility or civil liability, they're the easiest person to establish guilt, but they have the least money, and so workers get almost no payout from suing these folks." And, she explains, if you put one crew boss out of business, there are hundreds of migrant workers who would take his place because a crew boss can earn a little more money than the workers. But they have no control over how the system works.

Trafficking, Jean tells me, could be stopped if we had the political will to hold corporations legally responsible for the working conditions of anyone who labors in their business. "We can do that with the law," she says. "It is not that hard. We've done it in other sectors."

Sex trafficking, she explains, is also about exploiting people's labor. Young people wind up in sex trafficking not because a crafty man in a dark hoodie grabbed them from a parking lot, but because the other options they have are horrible. "Young people are lured in with promises of luxury goods or safety," Jean explains, "they're not being protected and valued in their own homes, and then someone else expresses interest in protecting them. 'Come live with me. I'll take care of you.' And often it evolves over time. So at first it's a clean house and running water and no screaming, and then several weeks later, it's, 'Oh, you have to perform.'"

"Sometimes it's very explicit," Jean says. "'You can come and stay with me, but rent is $300 a month, and if you don't have a job, I can arrange tricks for you, and then you can pay it that way. It's up to you, right?' It's not always explicitly coercive, but it is taking advantage of a situation where a young person is without better options."

"Sex work is very flexible," Jean says. "A lot of people enter into sex work because it is the job that fits their situation at the moment. And because sex work is criminalized, it's very hard to stay safe within sex work, because there are no OSHA protections. There is no minimum wage law. There are no protections against discrimination. So if you're getting into the sex work industry, you're working with a manager. If they're good, if they're bad, there's no one to complain to. And then people are stuck, because the reason they got into sex work is because they didn't have the money and they can't find a job. And now the criminalization of sex work has probably added new criminal charges to their record, which means they're even less likely to get a different job or to qualify for public benefits or affordable housing."

I asked Jean what she thought were the biggest problems with the public's understanding of human trafficking. She says that when trafficking awareness focuses on the most dramatic cases and the law enforcement response, then we miss the point.

Other than lawsuits, political change, and criminal justice intervention in the most high-profile cases, Jean says, the most effective way to address trafficking is to educate people who are most likely to be targeted. This is education that is best done by people that already have some trust and relationship with immigrant communities, or LGBTQ+ and other targeted youth. It's not helpful to put a sign in a bathroom stall at the airport urging passengers to call the police if they observe something that looks suspicious.

Also, when it comes to trafficking, Jean tells me, a lack of evidence is not the problem. This is different from most other areas of violence prevention. "We know everything we need to know," she says. Not knowing exactly how many people are being trafficked is not going to change the clear and obvious solutions. She worries, too, that commissioning yet another study is a stalling tactic. Jean reminds me that nobody would apply that standard to other crimes. "We don't need that level of exactitude in order to know what we should be doing about a crime. Do we know the exact number of muggings in New York City? Absolutely not. Does that mean we can't do anything about that? Of course not. We would never accept that. But for some reason with human trafficking, that keeps coming back up. 'Oh, we just need better prevalence studies.' I also am very skeptical of diverting resources away from victim services and into research that is unlikely to dramatically change the way people respond to it. I do think what we need to do is a better job of educating the public about what trafficking really is."

Like sexual assault, domestic violence, and so many other problems, trafficking has a helpline. Jean says that given the dynamics of trafficking, having one national phone number is crucial. "It is very important for victims to reach out for assistance and support, anonymously when they need to or to be connected to a local provider," she tells me, because trafficking victims are moved around and sometimes not told where they are going. This means they can't depend on local service providers in any one place, but having a national hotline to call could connect people to support no matter where their traffickers take them.

But, she says, the close connection between helplines and law enforcement impedes those who need them most. Because helplines for people who are being trafficked are often connected to the police, this prevents a lot of people from using them, especially if they are undocumented or involved in criminalized sex work. And since public education campaigns are so focused on "see something, say something," most of the calls to the helpline are random people reporting ribbons tied to cars or a sad-looking girl walking through an airport or a guy taking a nap in a dilapidated van. Meanwhile, a lot of people who are being trafficked and need support don't trust the police—some come from countries where nobody trusts the police. "We need to protect the hotline as a victim services hotline," Jean says. Random people who see something they believe to be trafficking can call 911 the way people do when they want to share other kinds of crime tips.

To be fair, some national news outlets do responsible reporting about the realities of trafficking. A 2022 *USA Today* article includes quotes from experts who explain that trafficking includes a complex process of gaining someone's trust, not snatching them from a big-box parking lot.[10] The Associated Press ran a story debunking a popular TikTok video about a baby seat being left in a parking lot as a ploy to lure women into trafficking.[11] It included quotes from an expert stating that most trafficking is done by someone the person knows and trusts, like a family member. But still missing from these more thoroughly reported articles is the clear but far-reaching economic analysis of how systemic inequity creates trafficking. And the reality that any of us, any person who wears clothes or eats food, may be benefiting from trafficked labor.

There's a particular type of disrespect that comes from labeling every scary parking lot encounter as trafficking. And the constant media focus on whether a middle-class and usually white woman did or did not narrowly escape being lured into a sex ring turns a problem that is clear and solvable into one that is so confusing and hyperbolic that we can't generate the political will to address it. We need the story more than we need the solution. And maybe I feel better about myself if I'm the person who gets on TikTok and warns other women to stay off their phones the next time they stop at Walmart. Doing this insulates me from having to acknowledge my actual relationship to trafficking—that the vegetables I stopped at Walmart to buy were only $2.99 because of trafficked labor. And that's why most media outlets and police departments can only debunk trafficking partway—enough to reassure a middle-class mom that she won't be forced into slavery, but not enough to face how deeply exploited trafficking survivors are and how much the rest of us benefit from their labor. Trafficking has become synonymous with "really bad crime," and because of that, our media and law enforcement are more concerned with reassuring those of us who will never be its victims than creating the structural change that will actually stop it.

ACTION STEPS

For Yourself

- If you hear or read something about trafficking, look it up before believing or forwarding it. Some fact-checking websites Jean Bruggeman recommends include polarisproject.org and factcheck.org.
- If you can afford it, buy clothes, food, and other products from small makers who have closer relationships to their supply chain. They are less likely to rely on trafficked labor.

For Social Change

- If your local news runs a story debunking a trafficking rumor and they don't talk about labor exploitation, write a letter to the editor or debunk it on your own social media. Put them in touch with advocates who can clearly explain why trafficking is a labor issue.

- Support (with time, money, or signal boosting) efforts to decriminalize sex work so that people who are in sex work against their will have more options to get out. Also, recognize that not all sex work is trafficking; seek guidance from sex worker activists to understand the difference.
- Support immigrant rights and workers' rights activism that will make people less vulnerable to trafficking.
- At the very least, support advocacy efforts that enable trafficking survivors to expunge their criminal records and get access to public housing and other services that exclude people with past convictions.

PART 4

WHAT YOU SHOULD ALWAYS DO

MYTH 10

"ALWAYS TAKE THE ELEVATOR. ATTACKERS HIDE OUT IN STAIRWELLS."

In the summer of 2024, I had a prickly email exchange with Mike McCord, captain of the police department at the University of Texas Arlington. It was about a page on their website devoted to safety tips for women. Why, I asked him, was there no corresponding page for men? Also, did the safety advice they gave women reflect actual crime trends on campus? How and why did they choose the directives they were giving to students?

The page was full of advice about what clothes women shouldn't wear, and where they should and shouldn't sit on public transportation. It also included a familiar directive telling women we shouldn't sit in our cars: "Women have a tendency to get into their cars after shopping, eating, working, etc., and just sit (doing their checkbook, or making a list, etc.). DON'T DO THIS! A predator may be watching you, and this is the perfect opportunity for him to take advantage of you." This advice, verbatim, can be found in several corners of the internet, including the police department of Rocky Hill, Connecticut,[1] a newsletter for office professionals who work for the US Department of Agriculture,[2] and a tourism publication based in Astoria, Oregon.[3]

Included in a long list of directives given to women but not men was "ALWAYS take the elevator instead of the stairs. Stairwells are secluded and provide opportunity for would-be criminals." But in the very next sentence, women were told, "Don't ride the elevator with someone if they make you uncomfortable."

Given that the biggest threat to women's safety on most college campuses is sexual assaults from people they know (usually other students, usually men), I asked the department why they gave this advice and, more importantly, how they expected women to follow it. Did they expect women to confine themselves to first floors? Or develop psychic powers that would enable them to predict who was going to get on the elevator with them and how comfortable or uncomfortable this person would make them feel? "Does UT Arlington have unusually high rates of crimes against women in stairwells?" I asked. "Is there other evidence that supports this precaution? Also, how do you help women on campus weigh whether a stairwell or elevator is safer given that a person on a later floor can get on and make someone uncomfortable?"

I got a two-sentence reply from Captain McCord. "UTA PD prioritizes community education regarding safety and security issues," he told me. "The crime tips contained on the UTA PD website are designed to help members of our community make our campus safer." In a subsequent email he declined to be interviewed.

When I checked back a few months later, the page I'd referenced was gone, replaced by a gender-neutral safety tips page that asserts, among other things, that "people" have the tendency to get into their cars and just sit checking their phones, not "women."[4] However, a simple search of the Wayback Machine turned up the original page.[5]

Warnings about stairwells, sometimes exclusively directed at women,[6] other times not, are all over the internet. They can be found in a workplace-safety brochure put out by the National Crime Prevention Council, an organization connected to law enforcement that is perhaps best known for giving us McGruff the Crime Dog. "Don't use the stairs alone," the brochure reads. Like the University of Texas, this advice is followed by a sentence that also cautions people about unsavory characters that can be found on elevators. The same brochure, almost or exactly verbatim, appears on the websites of police departments in Salem, New Hampshire; Joplin, Missouri; and Jasper, Indiana.[7]

There is no reliable evidence that elevators are any safer than stairs. Or even that any cluster of violence happens in either place, even in the FBI's national incident-based reporting system. FBI data doesn't separate stairwells from other areas in public buildings, but only 1 percent of crimes reported to participating police departments in the last five years took place in commercial office buildings, and less than 1 percent were in schools, colleges, and universities.

While some types of baseless safety advice cast our daily routines as dangerous, directives like this one go even further: they tell us to avoid activities that are good for us. The cardiovascular benefits of taking the stairs have been documented by credible research. In 2024, a meta-analysis of studies on the health benefits of stair-climbing was presented at the European Society of Cardiology.[8] Using studies that included a combined total of 480,000 people, the meta-analysis found that people who regularly use the stairs were 39 percent less likely to die of heart disease than those who don't. Other research has found that we don't have to climb a hundred flights a day to improve our health. A study in the United Kingdom found that people who climbed five flights per day reduced their risk of heart disease by 20 percent.[9] Benefits from stair-climbing can take effect as quickly as four to eight weeks.[10] Given that fewer than half of US adults get the recommended thirty minutes of exercise per day,[11] adding physical activity to our routines is a great option for people who don't have the time or money to join a gym. Stair-climbing is exhausting, sure, and not accessible to some disabled people. But it's a way to build wellness into our routines (not unlike other activities that are frowned upon in baseless safety advice, like parking far away from the entrance of a grocery store or mall so we can get a little extra walk while we do our errands). People's cardiovascular health is influenced by any number of factors, like how close they live to toxic chemicals or what diseases run in their family, but building physical activity into our lives is one option for improving our well-being.

As I reviewed the websites of law enforcement agencies and those of men who peddle safety advice to women, I compared them with those of health-focused sites that extolled the benefits of stair climbing. I found one defining difference: evidence. Every source from WebMD to the public health school at Tulane University to Harvard explained the evidence that supports the advice they gave.[12] In these cases (and so many others), legitimate health and wellness experts persuade us. They treat us like smart people who want good reasons for changing our lives. Policing often doesn't hold itself to that standard. While public health persuades, policing commands. Instead of treating us like our critical thinking matters, policing issues directives and expects us to comply just because they said so. Do this. Full stop. If you ask why, all you'll get in response is a generic two-line email.

Persuading respects our intelligence. It is rigorous and careful, it wants to empower us with knowledge so we understand why a particular lifestyle change makes sense. Persuading includes a healthy mix of confidence and humility—confidence that comes from knowing the evidence is clear and meaningful, humility that comes from believing that if we want other people to change their lives, we need to give them good reasons. Persuading not only gives people the specific information, but it helps them build critical thinking skills. Commanding, by contrast, asserts or affirms the authority of a person or institution and tries to belittle us if we try to ask why. Persuading respects us. But commanding, even when it is motivated by sincere concern, does not give us that kind of respect.

ACTION STEPS

For Yourself

- When someone is trying to get you to do something, pay attention to whether they are persuading or commanding. How does it feel to be persuaded? Does it feel different to be commanded?
- If you hold a leadership position at work, in your family, or in your community, pay attention to whether you are persuading

or commanding. Do you believe you should be followed solely because of your position, or do you feel a responsibility to give people quality information and reasoning if you want them to agree with you? Of course if you are a paramedic in a medical emergency, you may need to command in the moment. But as much as you can, try to be aware of the difference.

- Take the stairs if you want. Take the elevator if you can't or don't want to take the stairs.

For Social Change

- If your local police department, campus police department, or any government funded agency is giving safety advice without providing evidence, ask hard questions. This can mean reaching out to them directly or debunking the advice on your own social media. (I will never know if my questions were the reason UT Arlington took down its web page devoted solely to women, but putting an institution in a position of having to explain or justify baseless advice takes away some of its power.)
- If you are a campus administrator or you work for a company or government agency that publishes information about safety, ensure that your police department is not singling out women for life-restricting advice. Also make sure that the advice is accompanied by the best available evidence and if you can't give evidence or a rationale, don't include that safety tip.

MYTH 11

"ALWAYS TRUST YOUR INTUITION"

Intuition is one of the most difficult concepts in personal safety. Learning to trust ourselves, honoring our feelings and our reality is one of the most valuable actions we can take, not only to protect ourselves but to make decisions that give us joy and peace. At the same time, uncritically embracing every feeling we have can lead us to conflate our intuition with everything from racial bias to clinical anxiety. If we act on our first emotional reaction to everything, we could misread a situation in a way that harms other people. (Think of Amy Cooper in Central Park. She told a 911 operator that Christian Cooper was a threat to her when all he did was tell her the rules about leashing dogs in the bird sanctuary.) But if we dismiss or ignore our felt sense that something is wrong, then we may miss opportunities to keep ourselves or our communities safe. Abusive families and partners as well as toxic cultures constantly try to separate us from our reality, so trusting ourselves can be an act of resistance.

The biggest problem with intuition when it comes to personal safety is how often it is connected to blame: if you had a bad feeling and you didn't listen to it, then it's your fault you get attacked. The website She Travels Safely, a guide for women travelers, includes a post that illustrates this problem. It's written by a woman who was robbed while she was traveling in Brazil. She took a shortcut through an alley, where two men on a moped stole her wallet. "I did two things wrong and a third thing right,"[1] she tells her readers. "Wrong: I prioritized convenience over safety. It is easy to ignore safety tips in the moment. To cheat a little," she explains, "going the more populated route would have taken longer. I rationalized my way out of the warning to never walk on streets without people on them. Mistake number one."

The second "wrong decision" she described was not trusting her gut feeling. "Our bodies are evolutionarily wired to sense when something is off. Our gut alerts us in subtle ways: reoccurring thoughts, a sinking feeling in your stomach, or the hairs on the back of your neck. My gut was screaming that something was wrong in Brazil. I just didn't listen to it. Mistake number two." But even when she describes the thing she did right, it's really another way of making herself wrong. She asked local people she knew about common scams and was aware that a lot of robberies are committed by people on mopeds, but even though she was right to ask for information about local crime trends, she was ultimately wrong because she didn't follow the advice she got.

In his book *The Power of Awareness*, former military operative Dan Schilling gives us a similar narrative. He introduces us to Ashley, a single woman who was almost raped.[2] Schilling tells his readers that the reason this assault happened was because Ashley failed to trust her intuition. A man came up behind her as she was approaching the gate to her apartment complex and asked her to let him in. He was there, he told her, to visit a friend. He looked "clean-cut," she said, and "not your typical problem-type beach drifter," so she agreed, even though he gave her a look she described as "creepy." Ashley was in the laundry room later that night when the man came in and tried to rape her. Schilling described how fiercely Ashley fought back, how she yelled for help until neighbors arrived and stopped the assault. But none of that is the point he is using Ashley's story to illustrate. Schilling instead focuses on how wrong she was not to trust her intuition. He offers no analysis of why she, like many women, might not have felt she was entitled to refuse him. Schilling quotes Ashley as having said, "I didn't want to be a bitch and I thought it would be kind of ridiculous."[3] But what follows is not a discussion of how she got the message that saying no makes you a "bitch." Or how she learned that offending another person—even a total stranger—was such a serious infraction that it was worth subordinating her own feelings.

There's something blatant about the way Dan Schilling names gender socialization and then ignores it. My interpretation of Ashley's actions is that she felt a pressure to be nice that was so deeply internalized that she chose to accommodate a man who made her uncomfortable to avoid the possibility that even a total stranger might think of her as a "bitch." If she's like most people in this culture, she probably didn't get quality education about coercive control that could have helped her understand which behaviors are truly line crossing, so she may not have had a frame of reference for understanding her uncomfortable feeling. That she used his physical appearance to evaluate whether he was a threat only shows that most of the information people get about who we can and can't trust is based on stereotypes about people's looks rather than their behaviors.

Even best-selling author Gavin DeBecker, a trusted expert on predicting violence who has provided security advice and protection to thousands of people including celebrities, slides too easily into victim blame when he discusses trusting our intuition. Chapter 1 of his book *The Gift of Fear* starts with the story of "Kelly," a woman who bought too many groceries and was struggling to carry the bags up to her fourth-floor apartment.[4] One of the bags broke, sending cat food rolling down several flights of stairs. A man Kelly had never met offered to help. She had a bad feeling about him, but she didn't listen to it. She let him help her. He forced his way into her apartment and raped her. DeBecker has judgmental words for people who don't follow their intuition. "Instead of being grateful to have a powerful internal resource," he argues, "grateful for the self-care, instead of entertaining the possibility that our minds might actually be working for us and not just playing tricks on us, we rush to ridicule the impulse. We, in contrast to every other creature in nature, choose not to explore—and even to ignore—survival signals."[5]

"Every day, people engaged in the clever defiance of their own intuition become, in mid-thought, victims of violence and accidents," he continues, "So when we wonder why we are victims so often the answer is clear: It's because we're so good at it."[6]

DeBecker then directs his chiding of people who second-guess themselves exclusively at women: "A woman could offer no better cooperation to her soon-to-be attacker than to spend her time telling herself, 'But he seems like such a nice man.' Yet that is exactly what people do. A woman is waiting for an elevator, and when the doors open she sees a man inside who causes her apprehension . . . How does she respond to nature's strongest signal? She suppresses it."[7]

The concept of "women's intuition" is ingrained in our culture. It's imprecisely and inconsistently defined, but it usually has something to do with reading facial expressions, paying attention to other people's feelings, or anticipating the needs of men or children in a way that gets romanticized. But as journalist, author, and expert on emotional labor Rose Hackman has explained, there is nothing instinctual or primal about the extra labor a marginalized group does to appease a privileged group.[8] Especially when their livelihood or safety depends on being attuned to other people. Her work traces this concept back to a 1985 study led by psychologist Sara Snodgrass in which she randomly assigned students to either the "leader" or "subordinate" role in an interaction. She found that regardless of gender, the person assigned to the subordinate role took on more of the traits that are associated with being "intuitive." Subordinates paid more attention to leaders and therefore anticipated their needs, wants, and preferences without having to be explicitly directed to do so. Snodgrass coined the term "subordinate's intuition" to reflect this finding.

Subsequent research on intuition has focused on everything from identifying the brain science behind it to demonstrating its usefulness in the workplace. Intuition is generally understood as forming fast, unconscious impressions of new situations. There are often accompanying physical sensations like changes in heart rate that can get interpreted as "gut feelings." This ability to form quick impressions is needed when we are inundated with information and have to make good decisions with limited time.

Some experimental research has demonstrated the ways in which intuition is actually fueled by past experience. One example is a psychological test known as the "gambling task." In a study led by Oliver Turnbull, research subjects were given decks of cards that had high dollar winnings and even higher losses and other decks that had smaller rewards and penalties but were ultimately more profitable.[9] After repeatedly choosing decks and seeing results, subjects were more likely to choose the profitable decks and to choose them quickly without being conscious of the thought processes behind their decisions. This research also found that people experienced physiological stress responses when they approached the riskier decks. A 2021 study randomly assigned people to make hiring decisions either by trusting their gut and following their first impression or by carefully taking the time to thoughtfully consider the merits of each applicant. The results further supported the argument that intuition is actually experience and expertise.[10] Experienced hiring managers told to trust their gut or their first impression chose the candidates with the best qualifications, but college students with no hiring or management experience did not.

So a surgeon who has been practicing for twenty years catches a cancer before it spreads because she has a feeling about a tissue sample and sends it to the lab just in case. An experienced bouncer can't tell you why he thinks the guy in the corner is about to start a fight, but he was right, and he stopped it before it escalated. This is why intuition is especially ill-suited to matters of safety. Unlike the doctor or the bouncer, most of us don't have decades of good information to guide our less than conscious minds. Was Amy Cooper trusting her intuition when she called 911 on Christian Cooper? Was any white police officer trusting his gut when he instinctively shot a Black teenager?

My longtime collaborator Alena Schaim, the executive director of Resolve Violence Prevention, the IMPACT organization in New Mexico, has spent the past decade teaching people to differentiate between their intuition and other types of quick reactions to situations that don't help them assess their safety. Alena differentiated these unhelpful reactions into two categories: racial and other prejudices, and trauma responses that cause people to see innocuous events as threatening. To feel less scared, she explained in an interview, we have to be able to read situations more accurately. That way we can focus our attention on a person who could be threatening while not overwhelming ourselves by being afraid of the hundred other people who are not. Rather than avoiding certain neighborhoods because of racial or class prejudice or being afraid of all men because of past experiences of being abused by one or a few men, she teaches people to separate accurate assessments of the world around them from knee-jerk fears.

For people who have PTSD, Alena explains, it can be clarifying to have some criteria for what is actually cause for concern, rather than relying solely on an internal psychological or physiological stress response. Some trauma survivors have an overactive stress response that can be tripped by innocuous events (think of a combat veteran who "intuitively" runs for cover at the sound of July Fourth fireworks). She described why the blanket "trust your intuition" message can be frustrating for survivors. Especially for those who were abused as young children by parents, caregivers, or other adults they were supposed to trust. Having that trust violated, Alena explains, can have lasting consequences. "It causes deep interruptions in our ability to trust ourselves. So saying, 'trust your intuition, trust your gut,' to survivors just feels so unfair to me."

She described a student who had survived tremendous abuse who never got into an elevator with a man. One of Alena's goals was to present quality information about risk so that the woman could differentiate between her own visceral fear and the other person's actions. This could spare her the aggravation of avoiding elevators, but more importantly it helped her build the skills to identify danger. For other survivors who are avoiding dating, she gives quality information about what line-crossing looks like so they can have more fulfilling lives while still remaining vigilant.

Alena works to strike a balance, encouraging people to trust themselves, but also to use external information to check their first reaction. "We're pairing internal and external information," she explains. "That's where a lot of folks miss, is only looking at one or the other." This means honoring uncomfortable feelings we experience but also thoughtfully analyzing the external realities to see if they match. Not for the purpose of dismissing ourselves or avoiding the possibility of making someone else uncomfortable, but to make sure that we are distinguishing between innocuous situations and threats. Rather than not dating because some people are abusive, could survivors learn to pay attention to their date's capacity to respect their boundaries and use that information to assess whether the person is trustworthy? Rather than refusing to get into an elevator with a man because of past trauma, could a survivor learn to pay attention to the person's actions—Is the man in the elevator just another person with an appointment on the fifth floor, or is he standing too close to me, asking me personal questions, or dismissing me when I say I don't feel like talking?

"I want people to be able to trust themselves more," Alena says. "I think life is so much easier and more beautiful when we have that self-trust to navigate the world, it means that the world doesn't always have to be safe all the time, but if you know you can rely on yourself, life is more joyful."

One of the roles of quality self-defense is to help students develop intuition that is based on good information. Alena sometimes gives examples of situations that are not related to violence to help people become more aware of how they use past information to make decisions. One example she gives is a skier who has a feeling they should stop for the day. Rather than treating that feeling like some sort of superpower, Alena wants to help her students become aware of the knowledge the skier is using. "What were they observing? The snow was picking up; the ice was getting packed. So it was slicker. Their muscles were fatigued." So having this knowledge is one part, and then being aware of internal feelings is the other. "Intuition is putting together knowledge about how things happen with concrete things you can sense and describe."

Another part of trusting intuition is to disentangle it from the racist and stigmatizing stereotypes that so often provoke fear. A lot of personal safety advice, particularly when white women are the primary audience, doesn't encourage people to challenge racial prejudices, which devalues the people on the receiving end of those prejudices. Alena explains, "We can't trade some people's feelings of security for other people's ability to move through society without question and challenge, much less degradation." So if it makes white women feel better to clutch their purses every time they see a Black man, then we let the Black man endure that psychic harm so the white woman's intuition can be treated like unassailable truth.

If, instead, we understand intuition as a culmination of quality information and experience, then what we're really trusting is our best and most effective judgment.

ACTION STEPS

For Yourself

- Get lots of quality information about violence and safety so that your "intuitive" decisions are more connected to reality.
- Pay attention to the messages you've received about not trusting yourself. Who do they benefit? Pay attention to the messages you've received about trusting yourself. Who gave them to you, and who do they benefit?

For Social Change

- If someone talks about intuition as some kind of magical superpower, give the actual information. And if someone uses it as victim blame, push back.

CONCLUSION

HOW TO BE SAFE(R) IN AN EVIDENCE-POOR WORLD

Violence is a systemic and political injustice. Working to end it is critically important, but there is not total consensus, even among the most dedicated activists and experts, about how exactly we can change society to stop it. And even in the areas where there is consensus, there isn't political will, especially when the people who cause the violence are powerful or well liked. In this absence of evidence and political will, a lot of us, particularly those who are most targeted, are likely to stay safer if we take actions to protect and advocate for ourselves. "We keep us safe" is a common refrain of mutual aid groups.[1]

The last thing I would want to do is to give you a list of five or ten or even a hundred "easy" steps you can take to ward off the bad people. But there are smart, practical actions that each of us can take. Again, when I say be "smart," I don't mean "do what I say or else the violence you endure is your fault," I mean actually be smart. Think critically. Ask questions. Make thoughtful decisions that match your values and your lived experiences. Develop the intellectual and emotional fortitude to hold the complexities and contradictions of all the ways that people threaten and harm others. Do the best you can with the evidence we have and do the political work to advocate for the evidence—and solutions—we need.

Here are some specific strategies:

START WITH YOUR VALUES AND YOUR RISK TOLERANCE. Like any other type of risk, some people tolerate more and others tolerate less. Some of my friends still wear masks all the time, while others only do so if they've been in the presence of someone who has Covid symptoms. Some people zip-line, or bungee jump, and some people absolutely won't. Maybe you need to feel alert when you're on public transit or walking through a crowded city, so you would never wear headphones. Or maybe you're autistic, so if you didn't use headphones to cancel out noise, you'd be overwhelmed.

If your values include being an active bystander and speaking up when someone else is targeted for violence, it's important to make sure you have a clear idea of how much risk you're willing to tolerate to help another person and enough skills to do something useful in the moment. If you're on the subway platform and you see someone being harassed, what are you willing or able to do? Record the incident on your phone? Use verbal skills to de-escalate the harasser? Anything you want to do, make sure you get the kind of training that enables you to practice, so in the moment you have the presence of mind to use your skills under stress. Also, bystanders are not saviors, so make sure you have a way to assess whether your help is wanted.

TAKE A TRUSTING BUT CRITICAL STANCE TOWARD YOUR INTUITION. Sometimes we are socialized out of trusting ourselves and we dismiss our reality to avoid making others uncomfortable. Other times, we act on every feeling we have without stopping to assess the external world—is this person really dangerous or am I operating out of a stereotype or trauma pattern? As Alena Schaim says, pay attention to both internal and external information to help form an accurate impression of a situation.

BE THOUGHTFUL ABOUT THE DIFFERENCE BETWEEN STIGMA AND DANGER. Particularly for those of us who are white or have class privilege, we have had a lot of socialization that someone who is poor, or intoxicated on the street, is a threat to us. But if someone is not blocking us, yelling at us, getting too close to us, or trying to touch us without our permission, then our fear is likely driven by stigma and not actual danger. Also, some of the people who harm us the worst are well dressed, charming, and clean. So focusing on people's behavior rather than their appearance can make us safer.

GET HIGH-QUALITY SELF-DEFENSE INSTRUCTION SO YOU CAN BE PREPARED FOR UNEXPECTED SITUATIONS WITHOUT HOLDING YOURSELF BACK OR RESTRICTING YOUR LIFE. Even rare forms of violence happen more than zero percent of the time, so being ready is useful. There are ways of learning self-defense skills that will help you respond in the moment. My collaborator Lauren Taylor of Defend Yourself has created a helpful resource for how to find a good self-defense course.[2] Suggestions include looking for a program that explicitly challenges victim blame and understands abuse and violence as being connected to systemic inequities. Defend Yourself also suggests looking for a self-defense class that "respects each person's decisions on how to handle dangerous or threatening situations and doesn't blame or judge survivors. They will offer techniques, knowledge, and strategies to help students make their own decisions about how to handle situations. They don't tell students what they should or shouldn't do." Defend Yourself also recommends finding a class that "helps students empower themselves not only in the practice of self-defense but also in the program itself. For example, students should be free to decide their levels of participation in the class, and no one should feel pressured into doing specific exercises."

I would add the recommendation to choose a program that gives you the opportunity to practice physical and verbal skills in realistic simulations of harassment, threat, or assault. The human brain is not capable of making complex decisions under stress,[3] so when we are under stress, we default to our habits. Therefore, having some realistic practice helps us build habits that will serve us in threatening situations. We don't learn how to swim or ride a bicycle by watching a video; we learn by doing. The same is true for self-defense.

THE TRUE RED FLAG IS USUALLY A LOT SIMPLER THAN ELABORATE SAFETY ADVICE: PEOPLE WHO ARE A THREAT ARE THOSE THAT TREAT YOUR LIMITS AND BOUNDARIES LIKE THEY DON'T MATTER. This can be done by a stranger or a person you know, in a public place or in your home or office. The way to assess this is to communicate your boundaries and pay attention to how the person responds. Because of this, one of the most helpful skills is to practice communicating your boundaries in everyday situations, so it feels more natural to set them in a more escalated situation. If you lift weights regularly and then one day you have to carry something heavy, it's not going to be as difficult because you are used to lifting heavy things. If we get into the habit of communicating our boundaries, then like anything else we do habitually, it is a skill we can access in a stressful situation. Some of your boundaries could be not answering personal questions when they come from people you don't know well or don't trust, or not answering work calls or texts after hours. We are not obligated to entertain people just because they want our attention.

Another benefit of communicating your needs and boundaries is that you learn about the people around you—is someone in your life invested in making sure you feel good about a type of touch, a restaurant, a movie, or a type of sex, or do they just want what they want regardless of how it affects you? My coworker Shay Orent, who teaches teenagers about healthy relationships and has led a class for women on safe and sane online dating, described her own strategies for a *Washington Post* article.[4] When she matches with someone on a dating app, she sets a boundary right away. "It can be any boundary—maybe you want to chat on the app for a while before meeting in person or virtually. Then pay attention to how the person responds. Do they try to talk you out of your boundary? Do they try to find a sneaky way to get around it? Or are they invested in making sure you feel good and comfortable with the connection?"

Also, this is not just about your individual life (or it doesn't have to be). Speaking up and communicating boundaries (either yours, an organization's, or a community's) is a way to prevent abuse. Holding leaders accountable, insisting on transparency, all of these are steps that undo the absolute authority and silences that make sexual abuse thrive in institutions.

DESCRIBE THE BEHAVIOR THAT ALARMS YOU. Be specific. *You're getting too close to me. I said "No" and you didn't stop. You're blocking my exit.* Statements like these can clarify what line is being crossed. Much abuse and violence require secrecy. A person who tries to hurt us wants us to be too embarrassed or afraid to call attention to what they're doing. Naming the specific behavior makes it harder for this person to hide or deny their actions. For social change (and our own safety) it can be useful to do this even in nonemergency situations.

KEEP IT SIMPLE. KEEP IT LOUD. We don't owe someone who is harassing or threatening an explanation. Use simple phrases that state what you want: "Leave me alone!" or "Don't come any closer!" or "Stop!" It's OK to repeat yourself. If there's a bystander around who might be inclined to help us, yelling simple, descriptive phrases helps that person understand what's going on. If we are being recorded—by a person with a smartphone or an unseen surveillance camera—using phrases that make it clear that we don't feel safe can help us later if we need to establish that we acted in self-defense. Also, if you keep it simple and repeat yourself, you're not wasting energy on a complicated argument, energy that could be better used for making sure the person doesn't get too close to you.

The same with physical skills. It's not about being the Ultimate Fighting Champion or looking cool, it's about causing enough pain or enough distraction to end the threat against you.

IF SOMEONE GIVES YOU SAFETY ADVICE, ASK QUESTIONS. If they don't have an answer, the advice is probably baseless. If you're told not to go to the mall alone, ask if there is a documented increase in violence at the mall and if so, what types. Be critical of "common sense" if it's really just an attempt to make your life smaller.

Remember, critical thinking—not following the directives of a man with an authoritative tone of voice—is what it means to be *smart*.

ACKNOWLEDGMENTS

I have dreamed of becoming a published author for decades, but I could never have imagined writing two books in two years, much less writing two books in two years while navigating a nonprofit organization through this ridiculous and horrifying political climate.

I am truly blessed and duly grateful to have Leila Campoli as an agent. Leila, you are discerning, encouraging, and fully present.

Thank you to my editor, Haley Lynch, for being a strong champion and a thoughtful reader. Thanks to the entire team at Beacon Press. It is because of you that this book exists. Thank you for leading me away from all my misguided ideas, convoluted titles, and boring ideas for book covers. Thank you for knowing when to listen to me, and when to convince me to change my mind.

Specifically, thank you Marcy Barnes, Louis Roe, Alyssa Hassan, Frankie Karnedy, Caitlin Meyer, and Beth Richards. Thank you Susan Lumenello and Teddy Turner for a copyediting process that was a joy and a revelation. My capacity to misspell people's names is astounding, so thank you for catching every error and fact-checking every citation. Another hundred thank-yous to Mei Su Bailey, who does the essential work of collaborating with bookstores, and to Brittany Wallace for always answering all my emails.

Thank you to the executive directors of the other IMPACT Violence Prevention organizations: Donna Chaiet, Karen Chasen, Richard Chipping, Carol Middleton, Shanda Poitra, Alena Schaim, Katie Skibbie, and Martha Thompson. Thank you to my friends and collaborators in the empowerment self-defense movement: Lauren Bailey, Tasha Ina Church, Darlene DeFour, Coty DeLacretaz, Carmel Drewes, Kyren Epperson, Lindsey Falcon, Justine Halliwill, Julie Harmon, Jocelyn Hollander, Amy Jones, Brenda Jones, Ellen Krause-Grossman, Anne Kuzminsky, Brigit McCallum, Mark Nessel, Lindsay Orchowski, Michelle Pereira, Clara Porter, Kim Rivers, Candace Rushton, Clea Sarnquist, Susan "George" Schorn, Charlene Senn, Tasca Shadix, Silvia Smart, Lauren R. Taylor, Yuko Uchikawa, and Lynne Marie Wanamaker. I love working with all of you to find a way where there isn't one.

Thank you to the IMPACT Boston staff: Josh Alba, Autumn Buhl, Willie Burnley Jr., Ben Comeau, Kiki Ghossainy, Javon Goncalves, Sean Greene, Aaron Grossman, Michelle Morales, Alexander Nakhnikian, Shay Orent, Alicia Ortiz, Rene Rives, Elaine Sanfilippo, B Whitney, and Jeanine Woods. Thank you for rising to the political moment and keeping our enduring work strong. It takes patience and fear and despair to change the world, and I am honored to be working for that change with all of you. Thanks to our Turtle Mountain IMPACT family for bringing this work to Indigenous communities and showing us how IMPACT can be a force for decolonization, and the connections between body sovereignty and tribal sovereignty. In addition to fierce leader Shanda Poitra, thanks to Angie Decoteau, James Decoteau, Hunter Decoteau, Talon Decoteau, Dorothy Henry, and Loren Henry.

Thank you to IMPACT Boston's board of directors for meeting this political moment with integrity and moral clarity: Elizabeth Bostic, Claudia Castillo, Rania Henriquez, Keith Jones, Jorge Ledesma, Nancy Lee, Yuki Nishizawa, Janice Philpot, and Bonnie Tai. We are not scrubbing our website of references to trans people, anti-racism work, or anything else that is part of our core values, and I am thankful to all of you for treating that choice like the obvious right thing to do.

Thank you to Shaya French and Jules Patigian, the die-hard members of the Tuesday night writing group. What my heart would say if it only knew how to appreciate you for being patient when

I brought you draft after draft of the same few paragraphs. Thank you both for noticing the improvements, flagging the missteps, and helping me figure out whether something wasn't working or I was just sick of rereading it.

Thank you to independent bookstore owners and staff who give your communities moral clarity, historical perspective, smart political strategy, and much-needed healing in these times. Thank you for surviving and thriving despite the ways the business is stacked against you. It was a dream and an honor to talk about *The Cost of Fear* in bookstores, and you made that dream come true. In chronological order, thank you: Fountain Books, Harvard Bookstore, Women and Children First, Riffraff Bar and Books, Oblong, Blue Herron, Longfellow, Inquiring Minds, Symposium, and Porter Square Books. Thank you also to the Cambridge Public Library and Southwest Harbor Public Library. And thank you to generous and thoughtful conversation partners: Laura Bennett, Shameka Gregory, Nancy Lanoue, Lindsay Orchowski, Clara Porter, and Brandie Stringer. Thank you to Mirror Memoirs, Cambridge Women's Commission, the Meeting Point, Bonobo Sisterhood Alliance, Jane Doe, Inc., the National Women's Martial Arts Federation for sponsoring events, and Willia Vincitore, Professor Emerita Molly Shanley, and everyone else at Vassar College for a thirtieth reunion that was a true homecoming.

To my mom, Carole Stone, thanks to you I've never wondered if I was afraid when there was a challenge to take. Thank you to Arthur Susman for all the visible and less visible ways you've supported this book and the first.

Thank you to my friends who give me grace, support, and understanding. Thanks for your patience when plans came together at the last minute and your generosity the times I took over an entire brunch conversation with "fun" facts about the National Crime Victimization Survey or terrible safety advice on TikTok. David Pollack, there are no answers, but what would I do if you had not been my friend? Martha Thompson, your warmth, wisdom, endless gut checks, and academic library access have gotten me through the best, the worst, and everything else. Thank you to Patrick Calhoun, Roderick Ferguson, Ilene Fischer, Neil Savage, Amita Swadhin, and so many others. Thank you to mathematician and high school friend Chad Topaz for running a dozen statistical analyses of National Crime Victimization Survey data and explaining the results of each one. It is because of you that my capacity to bore people at brunch was at least mathematically accurate.

Most of all, thank you to my partner, Mal Malme. Mal, you have been the most supportive and generous book spouse a person could ever have. Living here in this brand-new world of writing, publishing, and resisting is only possible because of your loving presence. I admire your kindness, your sensitivity, and your heartfelt political engagement. When I think of home, I always think of you.

NOTES

INTRODUCTION

1. WFXT Boston Local News 25, "Timeline: The Amy Lord Murder, Investigation," August 6, 2013, https://www.boston25news.com/news/timeline-the-amy-lord-murder-investigation/140705164/.

2. A. Skylar Joseph, "A Modern Trail of Tears: The Missing and Murdered Indigenous Women (MMIW) Crisis in the US," *Journal of Forensic and Legal Medicine* 79 (2021), https://doi.org/10.1016/j.jflm.2021.102136.

3. Violence Policy Center, *When Men Murder Women: An Analysis of 2018 Homicide Data*, September 2020, https://vpc.org/studies/wmmw2020.pdf.

4. Martha McCaughey, *Real Knockouts: The Physical Feminism of Women's Self-Defense* (New York: New York University Press, 1997); M. Aziz, "Built with Empty Fists: The Rise and Circulation of Black Power Martial Artistry During the Cold War," PhD diss., University of Michigan, Ann Arbor, 2020.

5. Vanessa T. Marcotte Foundation, "Our Foundation," https://vtmf.org/about-the-foundation/, accessed July 22, 2025.

6. Vanessa T. Marcotte Foundation, home page, https://vtmf.org.

7. Annelise Mennicke and Katie Ropes, "Estimating the Rate of Domestic Violence Perpetrated by Law Enforcement Officers: A Review of Methods and Estimates," *Aggression and Violent Behavior* 31 (2016), doi: 10.1016/j.avb.2016.09.003.

8. Erika Harrell, *Violent Victimizations Committed by Strangers, 1993–2010*, US Department of Justice, Bureau of Justice Statistics, Special Report, December 2012, https://bjs.ojp.gov/content/pub/pdf/vvcs9310.pdf; Lot Guard, "Common Parking Lot Crimes," February 14, 2022, https://www.lot-guard.com/resources/blog/common-parking-lot-crimes/; Joe Curd, "Parking Lot Crimes and the Need for Robust Security," Stealth Monitoring, April 19, 2025, https://stealthmonitoring.com/crime-prevention/parking-lot-crimes-and-the-need-for-robust-security.

9. US Centers for Disease Control and Prevention, "Lightning and Your Safety," April 16, 2024, https://www.cdc.gov/lightning/about/index.html.

10. Shannon K. Jacobsen, "Gendered Responses to Fear of Victimization? A Comparative Study of Students' Precautionary and Avoidance Strategies in Suburban and Urban Contexts," *Violence Against Women* (2024), https://doi.org/10.1177/10778012241228284.

11. Chip and Dan Health, *Made to Stick: Why Some Ideas Survive and Others Die* (New York: Random House, 2007).

12. Jocelyn Hollander, "Women's Self-Defense and Sexual Assault Resistance: The State of the Field," *Sociology Compass* (June 19, 2018), https://doi.org/10.1111/soc4.12597.

13. Nancy Matthews, *Confronting Rape: The Feminist Anti-Rape Movement and the State* (New York: Routledge, 1994).

14. Judith Herman, *Truth and Repair: How Trauma Survivors Envision Justice* (New York: Basic Books, 2023).

15. Kris Bein, *Core Services and Characteristics of Rape Crisis Centers: A Review of State Service Standards*, 2nd ed., Resource Sharing Project, 2021, https://resourcesharingproject.org/wp-content/uploads/2021/11/Core_Services_and_Characteristics_of_RCCs_0.pdf.

16. Matthews, *Confronting Rape*; Beth E. Richie, *Arrested Justice: Black Women, Violence, and America's Prison Nation* (New York: NYU Press, 2012).

17. Pamela Mejia et al., *What's Missing from the News on Sexual Violence: An Analysis of Coverage, 2011–2013*, Berkeley Media Studies Group, 2015, https://www.bmsg.org/wp-content/uploads/2015/09/bmsg_issue22_sexual_violence_news.pdf.

18. Mimi E. Kim, "The Carceral Creep: Gender-Based Violence, Race, and the Expansion of the Punitive State, 1973–1983," *Social Problems* 67, no. 2 (May 2020): 251–69, https://doi.org/10.1093/socpro/spz013.

19. Meg Stone, *The Cost of Fear: Why Most Safety Advice Is Sexist and How We Can Stop Gender-Based Violence* (Boston: Beacon Press, 2025), 24–26.

20. Sarah Maslin Nir, "The Bird Watcher, That Incident and His Feelings on the Woman's Fate," *New York Times*, September 9, 2020, https://www.nytimes.com/2020/05/27/nyregion/amy-cooper-christian-central-park-video.html.

21. *Today*, "Amy Cooper Made 2nd Call to 911 About Black Birdwatcher, Prosecutors Say," October 15, 2020, available at https://www.youtube.com/watch?v=L3662COVmn8.

22. Nadia Telsey and Lauren R. Taylor, *Get Empowered: A Practical Guide to Thrive, Heal, and Embrace Your Confidence in a Sexist World* (New York: Penguin Random House, 2023).

23. Aubrey Gordon, *"You Just Need to Lose Weight": And 19 Other Myths About Fat People* (Boston: Beacon Press, 2023).

24. Gordon, *"You Just Need to Lose Weight,"* xi.

25. Shahrzad Shams, "The Tradwife's Catch-22," *Ms.*, May 2, 2024, https://msmagazine.com/2024/05/02/tradwife-women-work-neoliberal-husband/.

26. National Rifle Association (NRA), *Refuse to Be a Victim: Student Handbook*, n.d., 7.

27. NRA, *Refuse to Be a Victim*, 13.
28. NRA, *Refuse to Be a Victim*, 24.
29. NRA, *Refuse to Be a Victim*, 25.
30. NRA, *Refuse to Be a Victim*, 31.
31. St. John Parish Sheriff, "Women's Safety Tips," https://stjohnsheriff.org/2019/12/23/womens-safety-tips/, accessed July 22, 2025.
32. NRA, *Refuse to Be a Victim*, 31.
33. Randall Waechter and Van Ma, "Sexual Violence in America: Public Funding and Social Priority," *American Journal of Public Health* 105, no. 12 (2015): 2430–37, doi: 10.2105/AJPH.2015.302860.
34. Danielle Kurtzleben, "Trump's Executive Actions Curbing Transgender Rights Focus on 'Gender Ideology,'" National Public Radio, February 7, 2025, https://www.npr.org/2025/02/07/g-s1-46893/trump-anti-trans-rights-executive-action-gender-ideology-confusion.
35. Bureau of Justice Statistics, *National Crime Victimization Survey (NCVS)*, latest data available 2023, https://bjs.ojp.gov/data-collection/ncvs#6-0.
36. Susannah Tapp and Emilie Coen, "Criminal Victimization, 2023," *Bulletin*, Office of Justice Programs, US Department of Justice, September 2024, https://bjs.ojp.gov/document/cv23.pdf.
37. Bureau of Justice Statistics, *National Crime Victimization Survey*.
38. US Department of Justice, *National Crime Victimization Survey: NCVS-2 Crime Incident Report*, July 2019, https://bjs.ojp.gov/content/pub/pdf/ncvs22_cir.pdf.
39. US Department of Justice, *National Crime Victimization Survey*.
40. Alexandra Thompson and Susannah Tapp, "Criminal Victimization, 2021," *Bulletin*, Office of Justice Programs, US Department of Justice, September 2022, https://bjs.ojp.gov/content/pub/pdf/cv21.pdf.
41. Elise D. Riley et al., "Violence and Emergency Department Use Among Community-Recruited Women Who Experience Homelessness and Housing Instability," *Journal of Urban Health* 97, no. 1 (January 2020): 78–87, https://www.ncbi.nlm.nih.gov/pmc/articles/PMC7010900/.
42. Jennifer Smith-Grant et al., "Risk Behaviors and Experiences Among Youth Experiencing Homelessness—Youth Risk Behavior Survey, 23 U.S. States and 11 Local School Districts, 2019," *Journal of Community Health* 47, no. 2 (January 2022): 324–33, https://www.ncbi.nlm.nih.gov/pmc/articles/PMC9119052/.
43. Colleen Cary Katz, Mark E. Courtney, and Beth Shapiro, "Emancipated Foster Youth and Intimate Partner Violence: An Exploration of Risk and Protective Factors," *Department of Social Work and Child Advocacy Faculty Scholarship and Creative Works* 161 (2017), https://digitalcommons.montclair.edu/social-work-and-child-advocacy-facpubs/161.
44. Bureau of Justice Statistics, "Hate Crime Victimization, 2005–2019," press release, September 13, 2021, https://bjs.ojp.gov/press-release/hate-crime-victimization-2005-2019.

45. Rachel E. Morgan and Barbara A. Oudekerk, "Criminal Victimization, 2018," *Bulletin*, Bureau of Justice Statistics, US Department of Justice, September 2019, https://bjs.ojp.gov/content/pub/pdf/cv18.pdf.

46. Rachel E. Morgan and Jennifer L. Truman, "Criminal Victimization, 2019," *Bulletin*, Bureau of Justice Statistics, US Department of Justice, September 2020, https://bjs.ojp.gov/content/pub/pdf/cv19.pdf.

47. Rachel E. Morgan and Alexandra Thompson, "Criminal Victimization, 2020," *Bulletin*, Bureau of Justice Statistics, US Department of Justice, October 2021, https://bjs.ojp.gov/sites/g/files/xyckuh236/files/media/document/cv20.pdf.

48. Meredith G. F. Worthen and Cyrus Schleifer, "#MeToo and Sexual Violence Reporting in the National Crime Victimization Survey," *Journal of Interpersonal Violence* 39, nos. 21–22 (2024): 4215–59, https://doi.org/10.1177/08862605241234355.

49. Arthur J. Lurigio and Monte D. Staton, "The Measurement and Prevalence of Violent Crime in the United States: Persons, Places, and Times," *Journal of Crime and Justice* 43, no. 3 (2020): 282–306, https://doi.org/10.1080/0735648X.2019.1656102.

50. Alexandra Thompson and Susannah N. Tapp, "Criminal Victimization, 2021," *Bulletin*, Bureau of Justice Statistics, US Department of Justice, September 2022, https://bjs.ojp.gov/content/pub/pdf/cv21.pdf; Alexandra Thompson and Susannah N. Tapp, "Criminal Victimization, 2022," *Bulletin*, Bureau of Justice Statistics, US Department of Justice, September 2023, https://bjs.ojp.gov/document/cv22.pdf; Tapp and Coen, "Criminal Victimization, 2023."

51. Thaddeus Johnson, "Violent Victimization Is Decreasing—But Not for Everyone," Council on Criminal Justice, October 2024, https://counciloncj.org/violent-victimization-is-decreasing-but-not-for-everyone/.

52. FBI, "Crime/Law Enforcement Stats (Uniform Crime Reporting Program)," https://www.fbi.gov/how-we-can-help-you/more-fbi-services-and-information/ucr.

53. Lurigio et al., *Journal of Crime and Justice*, 287.

54. Weihua Li and Jasmyne Ricard, "4 Reasons We Should Worry About Missing Crime Data," Marshall Project, July 13, 2023, https://www.themarshallproject.org/2023/07/13/fbi-crime-rates-data-gap-nibrs.

55. Ariel Hart, "Audit Finds Police in Atlanta Doctored Statistics on Crime/Figures May Have Helped City Get Olympics," *New York Times*, February 21, 2004, available at https://www.sfgate.com/crime/article/Audit-finds-police-in-Atlanta-doctored-statistics-2793032.php.

56. Weihua Li, "DeSantis Claims Florida's Crime Is at a 'Record Low.' But He's Using Incomplete Data," Marshall Project, June 20, 2023, https://www.themarshallproject.org/2023/06/20/desantis-florida-crime-rate-incomplete-data.

57. Crime Data Explorer, "Aggravated Assault," FBI, last updated January 15, 2025, https://cde.ucr.cjis.gov/LATEST/webapp/#/pages/explorer/crime/crime-trend.

58. Ira Glass, "My Lying Eyes: People Staring Squarely at the Truth, and Still Finding It Hard to Believe What They're Seeing," *This American Life*, NPR, aired May 6, 2022, https://www.thisamericanlife.org/770/my-lying-eyes.

59. "Sexual Experiences Survey (SES)—Victimization Version," https://amptoons.com/blog/files/koss_SES.pdf.

60. Mary P. Koss, "Hidden, Unacknowledged, Acquaintance, and Date Rape: Looking Back, Looking Forward," *Psychology of Women Quarterly* 35, no. 2 (2011): 348–54, https://doi.org/10.1177/0361684311403856.

61. Koss, "Hidden, Unacknowledged, Acquaintance, and Date Rape," 350.

62. Koss, "Hidden, Unacknowledged, Acquaintance, and Date Rape," 350.

63. Koss, "Hidden, Unacknowledged, Acquaintance, and Date Rape," 351.

64. Mary P. Koss et al., "The Scope of Rape Victimization and Perpetration Among National Samples of College Students Across 30 Years," *Journal of Interpersonal Violence* 37, nos. 1–2 (2022): NP25–NP47, https://doi.org/10.1177/08862605211050103.

65. RaeAnn E. Anderson et al., "The Frequency of Sexual Perpetration in College Men: A Systematic Review of Reported Prevalence Rates from 2000–2017," *Psychology Faculty Publications* 11 (2019), https://commons.und.edu/psych-fac/11.

66. Kathleen C. Basile et al., *The National Intimate Partner and Sexual Violence Survey: 2016/2017 Report on Sexual Violence*, Centers for Disease Control and Prevention, June 2022, https://www.cdc.gov/nisvs/documentation/nisvsReportonSexualViolence.pdf.

67. Basile et al., *The National Intimate Partner and Sexual Violence Survey*.

68. Basile et al., *The National Intimate Partner and Sexual Violence Survey*.

69. Centers for Disease Control and Prevention, "Methodology of the Youth Risk Behavior Surveillance System—2013," *Morbidity and Mortality Weekly Report*, March 1, 2013, https://www.cdc.gov/mmwr/pdf/rr/rr6201.pdf.

70. Centers for Disease Control and Prevention, "2025 State and Local Youth Risk Behavior Survey," 2025 Standard High School YRBS, https://www.cdc.gov/yrbs/media/pdf/2025/2025-YRBS-Standard-HS-Questionnaire508.pdf.

71. Marcie Bianco, "Statistics Show Exactly How Many Trans People Have Attacked You in a Bathroom," *Mic*, April 2, 2015, https://www.mic.com/articles/114066/statistics-show-exactly-how-many-times-trans-people-have-attacked-you-in-bathrooms.

72. *Guardian* Staff, "Inside The Counted: How Guardian US Has Tracked Police Killings Nationwide," April 11, 2016, https://www.theguardian.com/membership/2016/apr/11/inside-the-counted-guardian-us-police-killings.

73. Benjamin Din, "An Inside Look at *The Guardian*'s Effort to Document Deaths at the Hands of Law Enforcement in 'The Counted,'" Knight Lab, December 15, 2015, https://knightlab.northwestern.edu/2015/12/11/an-inside-look-at-the-guardians-effort-to-document-law-enforcement-shootings-in-the-counted/.

74. Jon Swaine, Oliver Laughland, and Jamiles Lartey, "Black Americans Killed by Police Twice as Likely to Be Unarmed as White People," *The Guardian*, June 1, 2015, https://www.theguardian.com/us-news/2015/jun/01/black-americans-killed-by-police-analysis.

75. "Abused and Used," series home page, *New York Times*, 2012, https://archive.nytimes.com/www.nytimes.com/interactive/nyregion/abused-and-used-series-page.htm.

76. Dan Barry, "The 'Boys' in the Bunkhouse," *New York Times*, March 9, 2014, https://www.nytimes.com/interactive/2014/03/09/us/the-boys-in-the-bunkhouse.html.

77. Joseph Shapiro, "The Sexual Assault Epidemic No One Talks About," National Public Radio, January 8, 2018, https://www.npr.org/2018/01/08/570224090/the-sexual-assault-epidemic-no-one-talks-about.

78. U.S. Trans Survey 2022, "Safety," https://ustranssurvey.org/report/safety/.

79. Denise-Marie Ordway, "Research Raises New Questions About Missing and Murdered Indigenous Women," *Journalist's Resource*, Shorenstein Center on Media, Politics, and Public Policy, Harvard University, April 26, 2023, https://journalistsresource.org/criminal-justice/indigenous-women-missing-unidentified-research/.

80. Urban Indian Health Institute, *Missing and Murdered Indigenous Women & Girls*, https://www.uihi.org/wp-content/uploads/2018/11/Missing-and-Murdered-Indigenous-Women-and-Girls-Report.pdf, accessed June 18, 2025.

81. Charlene Y. Senn et al., "Efficacy of a Sexual Assault Resistance Program for University Women," *New England Journal of Medicine* 372, no. 24 (2015): 2326–35, doi: 10.1056/NEJMsa1411131.

82. Jocelyn A. Hollander and Jeanine Cunningham, "Empowerment Self-Defense Training in a Community Population," *Psychology of Women Quarterly* 44, no. 2 (2020): 187–202, https://doi.org/10.1177/0361684319897937.

83. Jocelyn A. Hollander, "Does Self-Defense Training Prevent Sexual Violence Against Women?" *Violence Against Women* 20, no. 3 (2014): 252–69, doi: 10.1177/1077801214526046.

84. Clea Sarnquist et al., "Evidence That Classroom-Based Behavioral Interventions Reduce Pregnancy-Related School Dropout Among Nairobi Adolescents," *Health Education & Behavior* 44, no. 2 (2017): 297–303, doi: 10.1177/1090198116657777.

85. Charlene Y. Senn, Jocelyn A. Hollander, and Christine A. Gidycz, "What Works? Critical Components of Effective Sexual Violence Interventions for Women on College and University Campuses," in *Sexual Assault Risk Reducton and Resistance*, ed. Lindsay Orchowski and Christine A. Gidycz (Cambridge: Elsevier, 2018).

86. Krista Fultz, "Why We Don't Teach Self-Defense," 2025, https://www.genesisshelter.org/why-we-dont-teach-self-defense/.

87. Leanne R. Brecklin and Rena K. Middendorf, "The Group Dynamics of Women's Self-Defense Training," *Violence Against Women* 20, no. 3 (2014): 326–42, doi: 10.1177/1077801214526044.

88. Caitlin M. Pincotti and Holly K. Orcutt, "Rape Aggression Defense: Unique Self-Efficacy Benefits for Survivors of Sexual Trauma," *Violence Against Women* 24, no. 5 (2018): 528–44, https://doi.org/10.1177/107780121 7708885.

89. Darcy Shannon Cox, "An Analysis of Two Forms of Self-Defense Training and Their Impact on Women's Sense of Personal Safety Self-Efficacy," PsyD diss., Old Dominion University, 1999, doi: 10.25777/pb25-y427.

90. Steve Kardian and A. Clara Pistek, *The New Superpower for Women: Trust Your Intuition, Predict Dangerous Situations, and Defend Yourself from the Unthinkable* (New York: Simon & Schuster, 2017).

91. Kardian and Pistek, *The New Superpower for Women*, 4.

92. Kardian and Pistek, *The New Superpower for Women*, 5.

93. Kardian and Pistek, *The New Superpower for Women*, 5.

94. Kardian and Pistek, *The New Superpower for Women*, 1–2.

95. Kathleen C. Basile et al., *The National Intimate Partner and Sexual Violence Survey: 2016/2017 Report on Sexual Violence*, Centers for Disease Control and Prevention, June 2022, https://www.cdc.gov/nisvs/documentation/nisvs ReportonSexualViolence.pdf.

96. Dan Schilling, *The Power of Awareness: And Other Secrets from the World's Foremost Spies, Detectives, and Special Operators on How to Stay Safe and Save Your Life* (New York: Grand Central, 2021).

97. Schilling, *The Power of Awareness*, xiv.

98. Schilling, *The Power of Awareness*, xiv.

99. Jacqueline M. Drew and Sherri Martin, "A National Study of Police Mental Health in the USA: Stigma, Mental Health and Help-Seeking Behaviors," *Journal of Police and Criminal Psychology* 36 (2021): 295–306, https://doi .org/10.1007/s11896-020-09424-9.

100. N. A. Smith et al., "Keeping Your Guard Up: Hypervigilance Among Urban Residents Affected by Community and Police Violence," *Health Affairs* 38, no. 10 (October 2019): 1662–69, doi: 10.1377/hlthaff.2019.00560.

101. Kardian and Pistek, *The New Superpower for Women*, 37.

MYTH 1: "ATTACKERS CAN TELL WHO MAKES A GOOD VICTIM BY THE WAY THEY WALK"

1. Betty Grayson and Morris I. Stein, "Attracting Assault: Victims' Nonverbal Cues," *Journal of Communication* 31, no. 1 (1981): 68–75, https://doi .org/10.1111/j.1460-2466.1981.tb01206.x.

2. Grayson and Stein, "Attracting Assault," 70.

3. Ulysses Bernardet et al., "Assessing the Reliability of the Laban Movement Analysis System," *PLOS One* (June 13, 2019), https://doi.org/10.1371 /journal.pone.0218179.

4. Michael X, TikTok, https://www.tiktok.com/@i_am_mike.x/video/7282772498251271470.

5. Steve Kardian and A. Clara Pistek, *The New Superpower for Women: Trust Your Intuition, Predict Dangerous Situations, and Defend Yourself from the Unthinkable* (New York: Simon & Schuster, 2017), 24.

6. Angela Book et al., "Psychopathy and Victim Selection: The Use of Gait as a Cue to Vulnerability," *Journal of Interpersonal Violence* 28, no. 11 (2013): 2368–83, https://doi.org/10.1177/0886260512475315.

7. Stephen G. Michaud and Hugh Aynesworth, *The Only Living Witness* (Irving: Authorlink, 1999).

8. Sarah Wheeler et al., "Psychopathic Traits and Perceptions of Victim Vulnerability," *Criminal Justice and Behavior* 36, no. 6 (2009): 635–48, https://doi.org/10.1177/0093854809333958.

9. Christine A. Gidycz, "Sexual Revictimization Revisited: A Commentary," *Psychology of Women Quarterly* 35, no. (2011): 355–61, https://doi.org/10.1177/0361684311404111.

10. Gidycz, "Sexual Revictimization Revisited," 355–61.

11. Gidycz, "Sexual Revictimization Revisited," 356.

12. Jen Soriano, *Nervous: Essays on Heritage and Healing* (New York: HarperCollins, 2023), 44.

13. Lily Burana, "Elegy for Times Square," *Memoirland*, October 30, 2024, https://memoirland.substack.com/p/elegy-in-times-square.

14. Liz Grauerholz, "An Ecological Approach to Understanding Sexual Revictimization: Linking Personal, Interpersonal, and Sociocultural Factors and Processes," *Child Maltreatment* 5, no. 1 (2000): 5–17, https://doi.org/10.1177/1077559500005001002.

15. Jennifer Murzynski and Douglas Degelman, "Body Language of Women and Judgments of Vulnerability to Sexual Assault," *Journal of Applied Social Psychology* 26, no. 18 (July 2006): 1617–26, doi: 10.1111/j.1559-1816.1996.tb00088.x.

16. Rebecca Gunns et al., "Victim Selection and Kinematics: A Point-Light Investigation of Vulnerability to Attack," *Journal of Nonverbal Behavior* 26 (2002): 129–58, https://doi.org/10.1023/A:1020744915533.

17. Kikue Sakaguchi and Toshikazu Hasegawa, "Personality Correlates with Frequency of Being Targeted for Unexpected Advances by Strangers," *Journal of Applied Social Psychology* 37, no. 5 (2007): 948–68, https://doi.org/10.1111/j.1559-1816.2007.00194.x.

18. Lindsay Fulham, et al., "The Effect of Hypervigilance on the Relationship Between Sexual Victimization and Gait," *Journal of Interpersonal Violence* 35, nos. 19–20 (2017): 4061–82, https://doi.org/10.1177/0886260517713714 (original work published 2020).

19. Tania Luna, "The Body Language Myth," *Psychology Today*, March 8, 2020, https://www.psychologytoday.com/us/blog/surprise/202003/the-body-language-myth.

20. Richard Newman et al., "Non-Verbal Presence: How Changing Your Behaviour Can Increase Your Ratings for Persuasion, Leadership and Confidence," *Psychology* 7 (2016): 488–99, https://doi.org/10.4236/psych.2016.74050.

21. Michelle P. Martín-Raugh, J. Kell Harrison, Jason G. Randall, Cristina Anguiano-Carrasco, and Justin T. Banfi, "Speaking Without Words: A Meta-Analysis of Over 70 Years of Research on the Power of Nonverbal Cues in Job Interviews," *Journal of Organizational Behavior* 44, no. 1 (2023): 132–56.

22. Judith A. Hall, Terrence G. Horgan, and Nora A. Murphy, "Nonverbal Communication," *Annual Review of Psychology* 70, no. 2019 (2019): 271–94.

23. Amy Arnsten, "The Effects of Stress on Prefrontal Cortical Function," April 27, 2021, available at https://www.youtube.com/watch?v=pFrdkDcPbj0.

MYTH 2: "DON'T FIGHT BACK. IT WILL MAKE THE ATTACKER ANGRY AND YOU'LL GET HURT WORSE."

1. Samantha Balemba et al., "To Resist or Not to Resist? The Effect of Context and Crime Characteristics on Sex Offenders' Reaction to Victim Resistance," *Crime & Delinquency* 58, no. 4 (2012): 588–611, https://doi.org/10.1177/0011128712437914.

2. Pauline Bart and Patricia O'Brien, *Stopping Rape: Successful Survival Strategies* (New York: Pergamon Press, 1985).

3. Christina Dardis, Sarah Ullman, and Leanne Brecklin, "'It's Worth the Fight!': Women Resisting Rape," in *Sexual Assault Risk Reducton and Resistance*, ed. Lindsay Orchowski and Christne A. Gidycz (Cambridge: Elsevier, 2018).

4. Dardis, Ullman, and Brecklin, "'It's Worth the Fight!'"

5. Jennifer Wong and Samantha Balemba, "The Effect of Victim Resistance on Rape Completion: A Meta-Analysis," *Trauma, Violence & Abuse* 19, no. 3 (2018): 352–65, https://doi.org/10.1177/1524838016663934.

6. Jongyeon Tark and Gary Kleck, "Resisting Rape: The Effects of Victim Self-Protection on Rape Completion and Injury," *Violence Against Women* 20, no. 3 (2014): 270–92, doi: 10.1177/1077801214526050.

7. Rob T. Guerette and Shannon A. Santana, "Explaining Victim Self-Protective Behavior Effects on Crime Incident Outcomes: A Test of Opportunity Theory," *Crime & Delinquency* 56, no. 2 (2010): 198–226, https://doi.org/10.1177/0011128707311644.

8. Bonnie S. Fisher et al., "Assessing the Efficacy of the Protective Action-Completion Nexus for Sexual Victimizations," *Violence and Victims* 22, no. 1 (2007): 18–42, https://doi.org/10.1891/vv-v22i1a002.

9. Fisher et al., "Assessing the Efficacy of the Protective Action-Completion Nexus for Sexual Victimizations," 26, 28.

10. Lindsay M. Orchowski et al., "Resisting Unwanted Sexual and Social Advances: Perspectives of College Women and Men," *Journal of Interpersonal Violence* 36, no. 7–8 (2021): NP4049–NP4073, doi: 10.1177/0886260518781805.

11. Ráchael A. Powers, "Predictors of Self-Protective Behaviors in Non-Sexual Violent Encounters: The Role of Victim Sex in Understanding

Resistance," *Social Science Research* 48 (2014): 279–294, doi: 10.1016/j.ssresearch.2014.07.003.

12. Ráchael A. Powers and Sally S. Simpson, "Self-Protective Behaviors and Injury in Domestic Violence Situations: Does It Hurt to Fight Back?" *Journal of Interpersonal Violence* 27, no. 17 (2012): 3345–65, doi: 10.1177/0886260512445384.

13. Alisa Bierria and Colby Lenz, *Defending Self-Defense: A Call to Action by Survived & Punished*, Survived & Punished with Project NIA and the UCLA Center for the Study of Women, March 2022, https://csw.ucla.edu/wp-content/uploads/2022/03/DSD-Report-Mar-21-final.pdf.

14. TransFighters, *A Self-Defense Study Guide for Trans Women: Because the Stuff that Works for Other People Doesn't Work for Us* (Portland, OR: Microcosm, 2021).

15. Lindsay M. Orchowski et al., "Evaluation of a Sexual Assault Risk Reduction and Self-Defense Program: A Prospective Analysis of a Revised Protocol," *Psychology of Women Quarterly* 32, no. 2 (2008): 204–18, https://doi.org/10.1111/j.1471-6402.2008.00425.x.

MYTH 3: "I READ IN THE NEWS THERE'S AN ATTACKER ON THE LOOSE, SO I NEED TO BE MORE CAREFUL OUT THERE"

1. Go Local Providence, "Police Warn of Rapist at Large in Providence—Urging Residents to Lock Doors and Windows," May 6, 2022, https://www.golocalprov.com/news/police-warn-of-rapist-at-large-in-providence-urging-residents-to-lock-doors.

2. Elisa Shearer et al., "Americans' Changing Relationship with Local News," Pew Research Center, May 7, 2024, https://www.pewresearch.org/journalism/2024/05/07/americans-changing-relationship-with-local-news/.

3. Jeffrey Gotfried, "Journalists and the Public Differ on How Journalists Are Doing, How Connected They Are," Pew Research Center, June 14, 2022, https://www.pewresearch.org/journalism/2022/06/14/journalists-and-the-public-differ-on-how-journalists-are-doing-how-connected-they-are/.

4. Andrew J. Baranauskas, "Exploring the Social Construction of Crime by Neighborhood: News Coverage of Crime in Boston," *Sociological Focus* 53, no. 2 (2020): 156–76, doi: 10.1080/00380237.2020.1730280.

5. Jay Jennings and Meghan Rubado, *Newspaper Decline and the Effects on Local Government Coverage*, Annette Strauss Institute for Civic Life, University of Texas at Austin, November 2019, https://moody.utexas.edu/sites/default/files/Strauss_Research_Newspaper_Decline_2019-11-Jennings.pdf.

6. Matthew S. Levendusky, "How Does Local TV News Change Viewers' Attitudes? The Case of Sinclair Broadcasting," *Political Communication* 39, no. 1 (2022): 23–38, https://doi.org/10.1080/10584609.2021.1901807.

7. Stephen Battaglio and Matt Pearce, "Backlash Grows Over Sinclair Broadcast Group's 'Must-Run' Conservative Content on Local TV Stations," *Los Angeles Times*, April 5, 2018, https://www.latimes.com/business/hollywood

/la-fi-ct-sinclair-promo-20180405-story.html; Anonymous, "We're Journalists at a Sinclair News Station. We're Pissed," *Vox*, April 5, 2018, https://www.vox.com/first-person/2018/4/5/17202336/sinclair-broadcasting-promo-deadspin.

8. Andrew J. Baranauskas and Kevin M. Drakulich, "Media Construction of Crime Revisited: Media Types, Consumer Contexts and Frames of Crime and Justice," *Criminology* 56, no. 4 (2018): 679–714, https://doi.org/10.1111/1745-9125.12189.

9. M. Sacks et al., "Rape Myths in the Media: A Content Analysis of Local Newspaper Reporting in the United States," *Deviant Behavior* 39, no. 9 (2018): 1237–46, https://doi.org/10.1080/01639625.2017.1410608.

10. C. R. Gravelin et al., "Assessing the Impact of Media on Blaming the Victim of Acquaintance Rape," *Psychology of Women Quarterly* 48, no. 2 (2024): 209–31.

11. ESPN News Services, "Woman in Georgia Alleges Sexual Assault," ESPN.com, March 5, 2010, https://www.espn.com/nfl/news/story?id=4970050.

12. Gravelin et al., "Assessing the Impact of Media on Blaming the Victim of Acquaintance Rape," 218.

13. Gravelin et al., "Assessing the Impact of Media on Blaming the Victim of Acquaintance Rape," 218.

14. Jocelyn Hollander and Katie Rogers, "Constructing Victims: The Erasure of Women's Resistance to Sexual Assault," *Sociological Forum* 29, no. 2 (2014): 342–64, https://doi.org/10.1111/socf.12087.

15. Hollander and Rogers, "Constructing Victims," 343.

16. Hollander and Rogers, "Constructing Victims," 351.

17. Hollander and Rogers, "Constructing Victims," 351.

18. Hollander and Rogers, "Constructing Victims," 354.

19. Harvard University Police, "Community Advisory—Putnam Avenue Assault and Battery," November 15, 2017, https://prod-hupd.drupalsites.harvard.edu/news/community-advisory-putnam-avenue-assault-and-battery.

MYTH 4: "TREAT ANYONE WHO LOOKS OUT OF PLACE WITH SUSPICION"

1. Steve Kardian and A. Clara Pistek, *The New Superpower for Women: Trust Your Intuition, Predict Dangerous Situations, and Defend Yourself from the Unthinkable* (New York: Simon & Schuster, 2017), 45.

2. Children's Hospital of Philadelphia Research Institute, "Stimming: What Is It and Does It Matter?" last updated May 29, 2020, https://www.research.chop.edu/car-autism-roadmap/stimming-what-is-it-and-does-it-matter.

3. Amtrak, "Defining Suspicious Behavior," August 25, 2016, available at https://www.youtube.com/watch?v=KqwOAGxus6I.

4. David Perry and Lawrence Carter-Long, "The Ruderman White Paper on Media Coverage of Law Enforcement Use of Force and Disability," Ruderman Family Foundation, March 2016, https://rudermanfoundation.org/wp-content/uploads/2017/08/MediaStudy-PoliceDisability_final-final.pdf.

5. Laura M. Maruschak and Jennifer Bronson, "Disabilities Reported by Prisoners: Survey of Prison Inmates, 2016," Bureau of Justice Statistics, March 2021, https://bjs.ojp.gov/library/publications/disabilities-reported-prisoners-survey-prison-inmates-2016.

6. L. Gardner et al., "Law Enforcement Officers' Interactions with Autistic Individuals: Commonly Reported Incidents and Use of Force," *Research in Developmental Disabilities* 131 (2022): 104371, https://doi.org/10.1016/j.ridd.2022.104371.

7. Elizabeth Koh, "New Law Requiring Autism Training for Police Officers to Take Effect," *Miami Herald*, September 30, 2017, https://www.miamiherald.com/news/state/florida/article176348886.html.

8. Lauren Gardner and Jonathan M. Campbell, "Training Law Enforcement Officers About Autism: Evaluation of Adding Virtual Reality or Simulation to a Traditional Training Approach," *Journal of Autism and Developmental Disorders* (May 2024), https://doi.org/10.1007/s10803-024-06383-6.

9. Mark Follman, "Inside the Race to Stop the Next Mass Shooter," *Mother Jones*, November/December 2015, https://www.motherjones.com/politics/2015/10/mass-shootings-threat-assessment-shooter-fbi-columbine/.

10. Emerson College, "Share a Concern," 2025, https://emerson.edu/departments/student-care-support/share-concern.

11. Florida State University, "How to Assist a Student of Concern," https://dsst.fsu.edu/student-concern, accessed June 18, 2025.

12. University of Nebraska Lincoln, "Student of Concern," https://cm.maxient.com/reportingform.php?UnivofNebraskaSystem&layout_id=103, accessed June 18, 2025.

13. Katrina Dix, "Petition Asks for Charges to Be Dropped Against Linkhorne Middle School Student with Autism," *Richmond Times-Dispatch*, August 30, 2015, https://richmond.com/news/petition-asks-for-charges-to-be-dropped-against-linkhorne-middle/article_f5b4a9b2-b55a-5379-994b-42ced62982ce.html.

14. Susan Ferris, "Virginia Tops Nation in Sending Students to Cops, Courts: Where Does Your State Rank?" Center for Public Integrity, April 10, 2105, https://publicintegrity.org/education/virginia-tops-nation-in-sending-students-to-cops-courts-where-does-your-state-rank/.

MYTH 5: "CRIME IS AT AN ALL-TIME HIGH AND GOING UP"

1. Jeffrey Jones, "More Americans See U.S. Crime Problem as Serious," Gallup, November 16, 2023, https://news.gallup.com/poll/544442/americans-crime-problem-serious.aspx.

2. Bureau of Justice Statistics, "Criminal Victimization, 2022," https://bjs.ojp.gov/document/cv22.pdf; Susannah Tapp and Emilie Coen, "Criminal Victimization, 2023," *Bulletin*, Office of Justice Programs, US Department of Justice, September 2024, https://bjs.ojp.gov/document/cv23.pdf.

3. John Gramlich and Kirsten Eddy, "The Link Between Local News Coverage and Americans' Perceptions of Crime," Pew Research Center, August 29, 2024, https://www.pewresearch.org/short-reads/2024/08/29/the-link-between-local-news-coverage-and-americans-perceptions-of-crime/.

4. Zach Norris, *Defund Fear: Safety Without Policing, Prisons, or Punishment* (Boston: Beacon Press, 2020), 38.

5. Norris, *Defund Fear*, 39.

6. Samantha Michaels, "Oakland's Progressive DA Just Wants to Do Her Job. In an Age of Recalls, That Job Is Changing," *Mother Jones*, March 18, 2024.

7. Samantha Michaels, "Oakland's Merchant of Bad Vibes," *Mother Jones*, November 4, 2024, https://www.motherjones.com/politics/2024/03/pamela-price-da-progressive-prosecutor-recall-campaign/.

8. Frank R. Baumgartner and Sarah McAdon, "There's Been a Big Change in How the Media Covers Sexual Assault," *Washington Post*, May 11, 2017, https://www.washingtonpost.com/news/monkey-cage/wp/2017/05/11/theres-been-a-big-change-in-how-the-news-media-cover-sexual-assault.

9. Alec Karakatsanis, "What Is News?" *Alec's Copaganda Newsletter*, June 3, 2022, https://equalityalec.substack.com/p/what-is-news.

10. Geoffrey Cubbage, "Analysis: Chicago Outspends and Outstaffs NYC, LA on Communications and Public Relations," Better Government Association, October 18, 2022, https://www.bettergov.org/2022/10/18/analysis-chicago-outspends-and-outstaffs-nyc-la-on-communications-and-public-relations/.

11. Maya Lau, "Police PR Machine Under Scrutiny for Inaccurate Reporting, Alleged Pro-Cop Bias," *Los Angeles Times*, August 30, 2020, https://www.latimes.com/california/story/2020-08-30/police-public-relations.

12. Behind the Badge, https://behindthebadge.com, accessed July 22, 2025.

13. Joe Vargas, "Fear of Crime and Lawlessness Are Growing Across the Country," Behind the Badge, December 21, 2021, https://behindthebadge.com/fear-of-crime-and-lawlessness-are-growing-across-the-country/.

14. Keri Blakinger and Alene Tchekmedyian, "Times Reporter Was Leaked List of Problem Deputies. The Sheriff's Department Investigated Her," *Los Angeles Times*, July 20, 2024, https://www.latimes.com/california/story/2024-07-20/a-times-reporter-got-a-leaked-list-of-problem-deputies-then-the-sheriffs-dept-started-investigating-her.

15. Clifford Karchmer, *Media Relations and Police Budgeting: A Successful Equation*, Police Executive Research Forum, November 30, 2002, https://www.theiacp.org/sites/default/files/2018-08/Media%20Relations%20and%20Police%20Budgeting.pdf.

16. Karchmer, *Media Relations and Police Budgeting*, 15.

17. Radley Balko, "For Police PR Flacks, Quack Lives Matter," January 31, 2023, https://radleybalko.substack.com/p/for-police-pr-flaks-quack-lives-matter.

18. Alec Karakatsanis, "Police Public Relations Spending: Part 2," *Alec's Copaganda Newsletter*, February 28, 2023, https://equalityalec.substack.com/p/police-public-relations-spending#footnote-1-103524879.

19. Rene Ropac and Michael Rempel, "Does New York's Bail Reform Law Impact Recidivism? A Quasi-Experimental Test in New York City," Data Collaborative for Justice, John Jay College, March 2023, https://datacollaborativeforjustice.org/wp-content/uploads/2023/03/RecidivismReport-4.pdf.

20. Andrew Stanton, "Eric Adams Slams Bail Reform After Violent Attacker Freed from Jail," *Newsweek*, December 12, 2022, https://www.newsweek.com/eric-adams-slams-bail-reform-after-violent-attacker-freed-jail-1766534.

21. Rep. Elise Stefanik Official Webpage, "Stefanik Leads Bill to Counter New York's Failed Bail Reform, Support Law Enforcement," press release, January 13, 2023, https://stefanik.house.gov/2023/1/stefanik-leads-bill-to-counter-new-york-s-failed-bail-reform-support-law-enforcement.

22. Constance Grady, "How 70 Years of Cop Shows Taught Us to Valorize the Police," *Vox*, April 12, 2021, https://www.vox.com/culture/22375412/police-show-procedurals-hollywood-history-dragnet-keystone-cops-brooklyn-nine-nine-wire-blue-bloods.

23. Alyssa Rosenberg, "How Police Censorship Shaped Hollywood," *Washington Post*, October 24, 2016, https://www.washingtonpost.com/sf/opinions/2016/10/24/how-police-censorship-shaped-hollywood/.

24. *Hollywood Reporter* Staff, "John Oliver Criticizes 'Law & Order' and Dick Wolf for Unrealistic, Highly Favorable Portrayal of Police," *Hollywood Reporter*, September 11, 2022, https://www.hollywoodreporter.com/tv/tv-news/john-oliver-law-and-order-dick-wolf-police-portayal-1235217673/.

25. Color of Change, *Normalizing Injustice: The Dangerous Misrepresentations That Define Television's Scripted Crime Genre*, Norman Lear Center, USC Annenberg, updated abridged version, January 2020, https://hollywood.colorofchange.org/wp-content/uploads/2020/02/Normalizing-Injustice_Abridged-1.pdf.

26. Color of Change, *Normalizing Injustice*, 12.

27. Color of Change, *Normalizing Injustice*, 60.

28. Kathleen Donovan and Charles Klam, "The Role of Entertainment Media in Perceptions of Police Use of Force," *Criminal Justice and Behavior* 42, no. 12 (2015): 1–21, doi: 10.1177/0093854815604180.

29. Esteban Fernandez, "Copaganda: The Effect of Televised Portrayals of Law Enforcement on Public Opinion," MIT Political Science Department, Research Paper No. 2024-13, April 22, 2024, https://papers.ssrn.com/sol3/papers.cfm?abstract_id=4800782.

30. Norris, *Defund Fear*, 47.

MYTH 6: "DON'T WEAR A PONYTAIL. AN ATTACKER COULD GRAB IT."

1. Avoid and Stop Attacks, available at https://web.archive.org/web/20230321165849/http://www.selfdefenseforsmartwomen.com/AvoidAttack.html.

2. Kristine Babiarz, "Through a Rapist's Eyes," letter to the editor, *Fruitport Area News*, September 10, 2015, http://updates.fruitportareanews.com/2015/09/10/through-a-rapists-eyes/.

3. *St. Mary and Franklin Banner and Tribune*, August 30, 2002, https://www.newspapers.com/newspage/473776030/.

4. Marmik Gupta, "Through a Rapist's Eyes," post of Babiarz, "Through a Rapist's Eyes," posted December 2, 2019, at https://www.linkedin.com/pulse/through-rapists-eyes-marmik-gupta/.

5. Kasat Brown, TikTok, February 4, 2024, https://www.tiktok.com/@chasingkasat/video/7331783949204704558.

6. Brynn Baker, TikTok, July 22, 2023, https://www.tiktok.com/@brynnmariebaker/video/7258853175166405934.

7. Bureau of Justice Statistics, *National Crime Victimization Survey: NCVS-2 Crime Incident Report*, US Department of Justice, July 2019, https://bjs.ojp.gov/document/ncvs23_cir.pdf.

8. Keith Faur, "Parking Lot Attacker Cut Woman's Hair," *Omaha World Herald*, July 17, 1991, https://www.newspapers.com/image/889779756.

9. Paul Gustafson, "Man Fixated on Women's Ponytails Gets Sentenced to Jail Time, Counseling," *Minneapolis Star Tribune*, December 2, 1998, https://www.newspapers.com/image/195182527.

10. Carla Johnson, "Helping a Friend Survive Domestic Violence," *Spokane Chronicle*, March 6, 1989, https://www.newspapers.com/image/566603037.

11. Nick Britten, "My Hair Was My Pride and Joy. He Knew How Much It Meant to Me," *Daily Telegraph*, January 9, 2006, https://www.newspapers.com/image/753336372.

12. *Good Morning America*, "SeaWorld Curator: Ponytail Likely Caused Fatal Killer Whale Attack," ABC, February 24, 2010, https://abcnews.go.com/GMA/AmazingAnimals/seaworld-curator-dawn-brancheau-ponytail-caused-fatal-killer-whale-attack/story?id=9934382.

MYTH 7: "DON'T PARK NEXT TO A VAN (ESPECIALLY WHITE VANS OR VANS WITH TINTED WINDOWS)"

1. Cassidy Milan, "5 Things I Don't Do as a Woman Running Errands Alone," TikTok, August 23, 2022, https://www.tiktok.com/@cassidymilan_/video/7135102718980656430.

2. Female Safety, "Girls Don't Park Your Car Near a Van," TikTok, January 23, 2023, https://www.tiktok.com/@female_safety/video/7191767613502950657.

3. Magic Mike G, "Please Be Safe This Holiday Season," TikTok, November 22, 2022, https://www.tiktok.com/@magic.mike.g/video/7168883233260571950.

4. Rape Aggression Defense, Student Handbook.

5. Women Against Crime, "Staying Safe While Shopping: Tips for Women and Girls in Grocery Stores," https://womenagainstcrime.com/staying

-safe-while-shopping-tips-for-women-and-girls-in-grocery-stores/, accessed July 22, 2025.

6. Sun Lakes Posse, "Women's Safety," https://www.sunlakesposse.org/womens-safety.html, accessed July 22, 2025.

7. Desoto County Sheriff's Office, "Tips for Women on Staying Safe!" https://www.desotosheriff.com/community/tips_for_women_on_staying_safe!.php, accessed July 22, 2025.

8. NBC News, "Arizona Woman Saves Herself from Kidnapping with a Post-It Note," August 25, 2023, available at https://www.youtube.com/watch?v=RBsRkGWhfWQ.

9. KTNV Channel 13, Las Vegas, "Neighbors Recalls [*sic*] Woman Being Dragged, Kidnapped from Apartment," January 31, 2017, available at https://www.youtube.com/watch?v=k9Ts7WRt7Sg.

10. FOX 11 Los Angeles, "New Evidence Shared in 'Rape Van on Wheels,'" May 21, 2024, available at https://www.youtube.com/watch?v=7wdu0OTw3ak.

11. Fox 13 Utah, "Video Shows 10-Year-Old Run for Safety After Men Attempt to Lure Him into Car with Candy," available at https://www.youtube.com/watch?v=KpPLTHLPxlU.

12. WALB News 10, "Leesburg Police Investigate Attempted Child Abduction," March 26, 2024, https://www.walb.com/video/2024/03/26/leesburg-police-investigate-attempted-child-abduction/.

13. ABC30 Action News, "9-Year-Old Girl Safe After Being Kidnapped in Sanger, Police Say," February 22, 2024, available at https://www.youtube.com/watch?v=o4EDHDJEGZs.

14. Jeffrey Walsh et al., "Examining 19 Years of Officially Reported Child Abduction Incidents (1995–2013): Employing a Four Category Typology of Abduction," *Criminal Justice Studies* 29, no. (2016): 21–39, https://doi.org/10.1080/1478601X.2015.1129690/.

15. Paul Renfro, *Stranger Danger: Family Values, Childhood, and the American Carceral State* (New York: Oxford University Press, 2020).

16. Renfro, *Stranger Danger*, 2–3.

17. US Department of Justice, "Legislative History of Sex Offender Registration and Notification," SMART, https://smart.ojp.gov/sorna/current-law/legislative-history, accessed July 22, 2025.

18. Kristen Zgoba and Meghan Mitchell, "The Effectiveness of Sex Offender Registration and Notification: A Meta-Analysis of 25 Years of Findings," *Journal of Experimental Criminology* 19 (2021), doi: 10.1007/s11292-021-09480-z.

19. Renfro, *Stranger Danger*, 4.

20. Renfro, *Stranger Danger*, 4–5.

21. Renfro, *Stranger Danger*, 7.

22. Renfro, *Stranger Danger*, 7.

23. Renfro, *Stranger Danger*, 57.

24. Renfro, *Stranger Danger*, 51–52.
25. Renfro, *Stranger Danger*, 62.

MYTH 8: "MAKE SURE PEOPLE CAN'T SEE THROUGH YOUR WINDOWS, ESPECIALLY WHEN YOU'RE UNDRESSED"

1. Lawrence N. Nadeau, *Basic Physical Defense for Women: Participant Manual*, Rape Aggression Defense (2016), 15.

MYTH 9: "DON'T GO SHOPPING ALONE. OTHERWISE YOU COULD BE A TARGET OF HUMAN TRAFFICKERS."

1. Women Against Crime, "Staying Safe While Shopping: Tips for Women and Girls in Grocery Stores," https://womenagainstcrime.com/staying-safe-while-shopping-tips-for-women-and-girls-in-grocery-stores/, accessed July 22, 2025.
2. Big Nic, TikTok, https://www.tiktok.com/@big_nic1976/video/7339845819056639274.
3. Molllyydoll, TikTok, https://www.tiktok.com/@molllyydoll/video/7164107911982026027.
4. KatyIronman, TikTok, https://www.tiktok.com/@katyironman/video/7445736901836868866.
5. Maddie McQueen, "Local Police Warn Against False Human Trafficking Posts," ABC36 Local News, November 17, 2021, https://www.wtvq.com/local-police-warn-against-false-human-trafficking-posts/.
6. William Russell, "Police Say Facebook Post About Human Trafficking Case at Walmart Is Not Accurate, Did Not Happen in Midland," First Alert 7, September 22, 2020, https://www.firstalert7.com/2020/09/22/police-say-facebook-post-about-human-trafficking-case-at-walmart-is-not-accurate-did-not-happen-in-midland/.
7. Laura Damon, "Rumors of Human Trafficking at Newport Walmart, Motel 6 Are Unfounded, Police Say," *Newport Daily News*, January 12, 2020, https://www.newportri.com/story/news/local/2020/01/12/rumors-of-human-trafficking-at-newport-walmart-motel-6-are-unfounded-police-say/1913117007/.
8. Kim LaCapria, "Hickory (NC) Walmart Human Trafficking Warning," Snopes, August 6, 2015, https://www.snopes.com/fact-check/hickory-walmart-trafficking/.
9. National Institute of Justice, "Migrant Farm Labor Trafficking in North Carolina: Pinning Down Elusive Data," November 20, 2020, https://nij.ojp.gov/topics/articles/migrant-farm-labor-trafficking-north-carolina-pinning-down-elusive-data.
10. BrieAnna J. Frank, "Fact Check: False Claim of Traffickers Targeting Victims Through Markers, Shopping Carts," *USA Today*, August 26, 2022, https://www.usatoday.com/story/news/factcheck/2022/08/26/fact-check-false-claim-human-trafficking-pennsylvania-walmart/7905642001/.

11. Angelo Fichera, "Fact Check: TikTok Video Spreads Unsupported Claim of Human Trafficking Trap," Associated Press, October 14, 2021, https://apnews.com/article/fact-checking-741499781117.

MYTH 10: "ALWAYS TAKE THE ELEVATOR. ATTACKERS HIDE OUT IN STAIRWELLS."

1. Wayback Machine, "Crime Prevention Tips," https://web.archive.org/web/20230927112500/http://www.rockyhillpd.com/CrimeTips/Crime.html, accessed July 22, 2025.

2. "Safety for Women," *MASCOP News Notes*, February 2007, https://www.ars.usda.gov/ARSUserFiles/60000000/MidSouthAreaOfficeProfessionals/NewsNotesFeb07.pdf.

3. Pete Curzon, "Stay Safe This Holiday Shopping Season," Discover Our Coast, November 28, 2010, https://discoverourcoast.com/2010/11/28/stay-safe-this-holiday-shopping-season/.

4. University of Texas Arlington, "Tips on Staying Safe," UTA Police Department, https://www.uta.edu/campus-ops/police/crime-prevention/crime-prevention-tips/tips-on-staying-safe, accessed July 22, 2025.

5. University of Texas Arlington, "Tips on Staying Safe."

6. The Redhead Riter, "Alert: Safety Tips for Women," September 2009, https://theredheadriter.com/2009/09/alert-safety-tips-for-women/.

7. Town of Salem, New Hampshire, "Crime in the Workplace," https://www.salemnh.gov/373/Crime-in-the-Workplace; Joplin Police Department, "Common Trouble Sports for Businesses," https://www.joplinmo.org/522/Common-Trouble-Spots-for-Businesses; City of Jasper, "Community Crime Prevention," https://www.jasperindiana.gov/topic/subtopic.php?topicid=50&structureid=19, all accessed July 22, 2025.

8. S. Paddock, "Evaluating the Cardiovascular Benefits of Stair Climbing: A Systematic Review and Meta-Analysis," European Society of Cardiology Proceedings, 2024, https://esc365.escardio.org/presentation/279143.

9. Zimin Song et al., "Daily Stair Climbing, Disease Susceptibility, and Risk of Atherosclerotic Cardiovascular Disease: A Prospective Cohort Study," *Atherosclerosis* 386 (2023): 117300, doi: 10.1016/j.atherosclerosis.2023.117300.

10. Anang M. Ghosal and Baskaran Chandrasekaran, "Stair-Climbing Interventions on Cardio-Metabolic Outcomes in Adults: A Scoping Review," *Journal of Taibah University Medical Sciences* 19, no. 1 (2023): 136–50, doi: 10.1016/j.jtumed.2023.10.003.

11. Allison Auburey, "Elevator or Stairs? Your Choice Could Boost Longevity, Study Finds," NPR, April 29, 2024, https://www.npr.org/sections/health-shots/2024/04/29/1247532191/longevity-stairs-climbing-exercise-heart-disease.

12. WebMD, "Understanding Heart Disease," medically reviewed May 15, 2023, https://www.webmd.com/heart-disease/understanding-heart-disease

-symptoms; Andrew J. Yawn, "Walking More Than Five Flights of Stairs a Day Can Cut Risk of Heart Disease by 20%, Study Says," Celia Scott Weatherhead School of Public Health and Tropical Medicine, Tulane University, https://sph.tulane.edu/walking-more-five-flights-stairs-day-can-cut-risk-heart-disease-20-study-says, accessed July 22, 2025; Julie Corliss, "Climbing Stairs Linked to Lower Risk of Heart Disease," *Harvard Heart Letter*, December 1, 2023, https://www.health.harvard.edu/heart-health/climbing-stairs-linked-to-lower-risk-of-heart-disease.

MYTH II: "ALWAYS TRUST YOUR INTUITION"

1. She Travels Safely, "Use Your Intuition to Stay Safe Traveling Alone," September 22, 2023, https://shetravelssafely.com/intuition-and-solo-female-travel/.

2. Dan Schilling, *The Power of Awareness: And Other Secrets from the World's Foremost Spies, Detectives, and Special Operators on How to Stay Safe and Save Your Life* (New York: Grand Central, 2021), 39–40.

3. Schilling, *The Power of Awareness*, 40.

4. Gavin DeBecker, *The Gift of Fear: Survival Signals That Protect Us from Violence* (New York: Little Brown, 1997).

5. DeBecker, *The Gift of Fear*, 32.

6. DeBecker, *The Gift of Fear*, 33.

7. DeBecker, *The Gift of Fear*, 33.

8. Victoria Vouloumanos, "According to Psychology, Women's Intuition Is Actually Subordinate's Intuition. Here's What That Means," *BuzzFeed*, February 23, 2024, https://www.buzzfeed.com/victoriavouloumanos/womens-intuition-emotional-labor.

9. Oliver H. Turnbull et al., "Emotion-Based Learning: Insights from the Iowa Gambling Task," *Frontiers in Psychology* 5 (March 21, 2014): 162, https://www.ncbi.nlm.nih.gov/pmc/articles/PMC3968745/.

10. Vinod U. Vincent et al., "Should You Follow Your Gut? The Impact of Expertise on Intuitive Hiring Decisions for Complex Jobs," *Journal of Management & Organization* 30, no. 4 (July 2024): 910–30, https://www.cambridge.org/core/journals/journal-of-management-and-organization/article/should-you-follow-your-gut-the-impact-of-expertise-on-intuitive-hiring-decisions-for-complex-jobs/0CFF8B1885FA549C6AFFCF082AC55E4B.

CONCLUSION

1. Community Resource Hub, "We Keep Us Safe: Mutual Aid How-To," https://communityresourcehub.org/resource/we-keep-us-safe-mutual-aid-how-to/, accessed July 22, 2025.

2. Defend Yourself, "How to Pick and Empowerment Self-Defense Class," https://defendyourself.org/whats-a-class-like/picking-a-self-defense-class/, accessed July 22, 2025.

3. Amy Arnsten, "The Effects of Stress on Prefrontal Cortical Function," CSSA Berkeley, April 27, 2021, available at https://www.youtube.com/watch?v=pFrdkDcPbj0.

4. Janay Kingsbury, "Self-Defense Can Be Hard to Remember Under Stress, Here Are 9 Easy Tips from Experts, *Washington Post*, August 14, 2021, https://www.washingtonpost.com/gender-identity/self-defense-can-be-hard-to-remember-under-stress-here-are-9-easy-tips-from-experts/.

INDEX

abduction: likely perpetrators, 137–38; parental fears about, 138–39; from parking lots, 134–35; trunk abductions, 15; and on white victims, 140. *See also* parking lot violence
ableism, 93–96, 100, 103
abuse history, 2–7, 10, 12, 50–53, 56–57, 60, 70, 73, 94, 137–38, 142, 153, 174, 179
Adams, Eric, 114
agricultural workers, trafficking of, 153–54
Amtrak safety video, 92
Annenberg Norman Lear Center, data about police TV shows, 116
anti-Asian violence, 22
Associated Press, on erroneous TikTok messages, 157
"Attracting Assault: Victims' Nonverbal Cues" (Stein and Grayson), 45–47
autistic people: associated behaviors, 91–93, 103–4; fear of, 78–79; police responses to, 93–95; stigmatizing of, 96–99; stimming by, 95–96, 103. *See also* ableism; Moon-Robinson, Kayleb
Autistic Self-Advocacy Network (ASAN), 91–93, 100–101
bail reform, 113–14
Baker, Brynn, 127
Balash, Josh, 107
Balemba, Samantha, 66
Balko, Radley, 112
Baltazar, Patrick, 140
Baranauskas, Andrew, 80–82
Barry, Dan, 33
Bart, Pauline, 64
Basile, Kathleen, 28–29
Behind the Badge website, 110–11
Better Government Association, 109
Big Nic TikTok safety videos, 150
Black people, victimization, 2, 23, 140
Bland, Sandra, 92
body language, 45, 51–52, 56, 58, 71. *See also* "victim walk" studies
Book, Angela, 47–49, 57
Boston Globe: reporting on crime, 80; victim-blaming in, 82–84
Boudin, Chesa, 108
boundaries: being specific, 144, 181; recognizing and communicating, 180–81
Brancheau, Dawn, 129
Brown, Kasat, 127
Brown, Michael, 32
Bruggeman, Jean, 151–58
Burana, Lily, 52
Bureau of Justice Statistics data, 19–20, 106, 121, 135, 146

Canada, Flip the Script program, 35
Catholic Church, sexual abuse and, 38–39
Centers for Disease Control and Prevention (CDC), on prevalence of intimate partner violence, 28–30
Charlotte-Mecklenburg Police Department, 112
child abductions. *See* abduction
children: data on abusers, 137; empowering, 141–44; empowering, approaches to, 141–43; resistance by, 140–41
clothing: equating modesty with safety, 146–47; fearmongering about, 53–54, 56, 126, 151; impacts on
coercive control, 12–13, 17, 41–42, 52, 171
college campuses, sexual assault on, 26, 50, 53, 164
Color of Change, 116
commanding vs. persuading, 166
Cooper, Amy, 12, 173
Cooper, Christian, 12, 173
Copaganda newsletter (Karakatsanis), 109
The Counted database, 32
crime: crime dramas, 115–18; defining, 113; incidence data, 106; myths about, 7–9, 105–7, 120; statistical data on, 80–82
critical thinking: asking for evidence, 167; about crime statistics, 120–21; about police shows, 121; about ponytail warnings, 131; and problem-solving skills, 129; and recognizing baseless safety advice, 11–13, 42; recognizing personal prejudices, 175; trusting your intuition, 175–76; value of, for self-protection, 60
Cubbage, Geoffrey, 109
Data Collaborative for Justice, 113
Davis, Mike, 115
DeBecker, Gavin, 171–72
Defend Yourself, 178
Defending Self-Defense: A Call to Action by Survived & Punished (UCLA Center for the Study of Women), 70–71
Defund Fear (Norris), 107, 120
DeSoto County (Florida) Sheriff's Office, 134
Diallo, Amadou, 111
disabled people: the criminalization of difference, 92, 95–96; learning about behaviors of, 103–4; as survivors of abuse, 31, 33. *See also* ableism; autistic people
domestic violence. *See* intimate partner violence
Donovan Kathleen, 117
Doss, Stacy, 100
Dragnet (TV show), 114–15
Drakulich, Kevin, 81–82
drug users, as survivors of abuse, 70–71

"Elegy for Times Square" (Burana), 52
elevators, warnings about, 163–65, 167, 172
empowerment narratives, 14–15
Enhanced Access, Acknowledge, Act (EAAA) program, 35
entertainment media, police-themed programs, 114–20

factcheck.org, 158
farm workers, trafficking of, 154
fatphobia, 13
FBI, crime data, 24–26, 96,165
FBI (TV show), 115
fearmongering: as architects of anxiety, 107; and beliefs about crime, 120; and campaigns

against bail reform, 114; impact of police shows, 118; as a political tactic, 107–9; ponytail warnings, 126–27; and safety directives for women only, 163–64; about threats to bodily safety, 108
Fernandez, Esteban Manual, 118
"fighting back." *See* victim resistance
Firecracker Foundation, 142
Fisher, Bonnie, 67–68
Flip the Script program, Canada, 35
Follman, Mark, 96
forceful physical and verbal resistance, 65. *See also* resistance
foster care system, 21–22
freeze responses, 50, 61, 63
Fulham, Lindsay, 57–58

Garbarino Andrew, 114
Gardner, Lauren, 94–95
Genay, Michael, 134
gender discrimination: and gender-neutral safety tips, 164; within police departments, 9; and resistance challenges, 3; on television shows, 117; and "women's empowerment" memes, 13–14
gender-neutral safety tips, 164
Get Empowered: A Practical Guide... (Telsey and Taylor), 13
Gidycz, Christine, 36, 50–53, 72
The Gift of Fear (DeBecker), 171–72
Giuliani, Rudy, 105
Glick, Harry, 125
Gordon, Aubrey, 13
Gordon, Laurie, 141–42
Grady, Constance, 114–15
Grauerholz, Liz, 53
Gravelin, Claire, 82–84, 86
Gray, Freddie, 92
Grayson, Betty, 46–47
Gross, Zoe, 91–93, 95, 97
group homes for disabled adults, abuse in, 33
The Guardian, The Counted database, 32
Guerette, Rob, 66–67
Gunns, Rebecca, 55

Hackman, Rose, 172
Hakim, Danny, 33
Hall Judith, 59
Hartford Courant, coverage of student sexual assault, 84–85
Heath, Chip and Dan, 7–9
helplines, 156–57
"hero cop" persona. *See* police
Highway Patrol (TV show), 115
Hoffman, Trish, 149
Hollander, Jocelyn, 35–36, 84–86
homeless people, vulnerability, 22
homicides, demographics of, 2
hypervigilance: defined, 41–42; fearmongering and, 107–8; as a result of trauma, 41; and unconscious reactions, 107. *See* abuse history; trauma experiences

IMPACT Boston, 6, 130
Indigenous women, violence against, 2, 34
intimate partner violence: and homicide rates, 2; incidence, 9, 27–28; studies involving, 101–2. *See also* coercive control; perpetrators
intuition: helpful vs. unhelpful reactions, 173–76; and integrating external information, 174–75, 178; and past experiences, 172, 173, 175–76; in personal safety directives, 169–72

janitorialwatch.org, 121–22
John Jay College of Criminal Justice, City University of NY, Data Collaborative for Justice, 113
Johnston, Lucy, 55

Karakatsanis, Alec, 108–9, 112
Kardian, Steve, 37–40, 42, 47, 91
Keystone Cops, 114
kidnapping. *See* abduction
Kleck, Gary, 66
Knight, Raymond, 64–65
Koss, Mary, 26–29, 35, 50

Laban movement analysis, 46–47
Lau, Maya, 109–11
Law and Order franchise, 115–16, 118–20
Levendusky, Matthew, 80–81
LGBTQ+ community, vulnerability to trafficking, 153
local news, as information source, 80, 86–87
Los Angeles Times, report on police spending on PR, 109–11
Louima, Abner, 111
Louisiana Sheriff's Association, safety tips for women, 15
Lurigio, Arthur, 23

Maintenance Cooperation Trust Fund (MCTF), 121–22
male protectors, subordinating to, as way of achieving personal safety, 13–14
Marcotte, Vanessa, 4
marginalized groups, vulnerability, 70–71, 92
Marshall Project, 122
mass incarceration, 139
mass shootings, risk factors for, 96
McCord, Mike, 163
Media Relations and Police Budgeting: A Successful Equation (Police Executive Research Forum), 111–12
Mehrabian, Albert, 58
#MeToo movement, 22, 24, 26, 33, 77, 87
Michaels, Samantha, 107–8
Michael X, 47
Milan, Cassidy, 133
modesty, equating with safety, 146–47
Moon-Robinson, Kayleb, 97–101
Murzynski, Jennifer, 53–54

Nadeau, Lawrence, 36
National Crime Prevention Council safety tips, 164
National Crime Victimization Survey (NCVS): annual reports, 121; benefits of, 23–24; biases and limitations of findings, 21–24; data from, 19–21, 66–67, 106, 121, 128
National Incident-Based Reporting System (NIBRS, FBI), 19–20, 24–26, 137–38
National Institute of Justice, 153–54
National Intimate Partner and Sexual Violence Survey (NISVS), 28–30
National Rifle Association (NRA), Refuse to Be a Victim course, 14–15, 16
NCVS. *See* National Crime Victimization Survey (NCVS)
Nervous (Soriano), 51–52
news media: applying critical thinking to, 88–89; challenging biases, identifying news sources, 121; newspapers.com, 128–29; researching, 89; underreporting of resistance, 85
The New Superpower for Women (Kardian), 37–39, 47, 91
New York City Police Department, PR, 111–12
New York Post, victim-blaming in sexual assault coverage, 82–84
New York State, bail reform legislation, 113

New York Times, on abuse in group homes abuse in NY group homes, 33
NIBRS. *See* National Incident-Based Reporting System (NIBRS, FBI)
nonforceful physical resistance, 65, 67–68, 70
nonsexual assaults, 69–70
nonverbal communication: becoming aware of, 61; studies of, 57–59
Norris, Zach, 107, 120

O'Brien, Patricia, 64
Onaiwu, Morénike Giwa, 97–101
Orchowski, Lindsay, 68–69, 72
Orent, Shay, 180
othering, 97–99, 101–3. *See also* stranger danger messages

Parker, William H., 115
parking lot violence: data about, 135–36; and stranger danger messages, 134–38; warnings about, 133–35. *See also* abduction
perpetrators: diversity of, 60; as familiar, 50, 52–53, 67, 78–80, 101–2, 137; victim identification studies, 50–56. *See also* intimate partner violence; stranger danger messages
personal safety: countering erroneous assumptions, 3–4, 10; life-restricting vs. useful warnings, 166–71; separating fact from fiction, 16; subjective factors, 121; systemic issues, 16; traditionalist approaches, 1–7. *See also* fearmongering; intuition
persuading vs. commanding, 166
Pew Research Center, analysis of public misperception of crime incidence, 106–7
physical appearance, 54, 58, 83, 178
point-light analysis studies, 54–55
polarisproject.org, 158
police: documenting encounters with 104; equating difference with danger, 97–98; as experts on violence, crime, and safety, 9; "hero cop" persona, 114–20; law-and-order policies, 139; Rape Aggression Defense (RAD) program, 36–37; response to autistic and disabled people, 92–94; and stigma associated with mental health services, 40; trafficking claims, 150–51; violence associated with, coverups/PR, 3, 32–33, 100, 109–12, 115–18, 122; warnings by, critiques, 134, 163–67
Police Executive Research Forum report, 111–12
ponytail warnings, 125–29
post-traumatic stress disorder (PTSD), 40–42, 50–51, 174
The Power of Awareness (Schilling), 39, 170
Powers, Ráchael, 69–70
"Predator vs. Ponytail" (video, Baker), 127
predators. *See* perpetrators; intimate partner violence
Price, Pamela, 108
problem-solving skills, 129. *See also* critical thinking
PTSD (post-traumatic stress disorder), 40–42, 50–51, 174
public bathrooms, safety of, 31–32

racism: and ableism, 100, 103; and feeling unsafe, 121; promoting through safety directives, 10–12; safety advice that perpetuates, 11–12; and stranger

danger messages, 140; and unhelpful reactions to threatening situations, 174; violence resulting from, 177
Raffle, Holly, 72
Rams, Bill, 110
rape, as a term, 27. *See also* sexual violence
Rape Aggression Defense (RAD), 14, 36–37, 134, 145
Refuse to Be a Victim course (NRA), 14–15
Rempel Michael, 113
Renfro, Paul, 138–40
resistance: by children, 140–41; effectiveness of, 64–69, 71–72, 84–86; punishment for, 73; underreporting of, 85–86; yelling, shouting, 65, 69, 129–30, 133, 181. *See also* verbal resistance; victim resistance
risk tolerance, 178
Robertson, Nicholas, 110
Rodger, Elliot, 96
Rogers, Katie, 84–86
Ropac, Rene, 113
Rosenberg, Alyssa, 115–16

Sacks, Meghan, 82
safety advice: baseless, characteristics, 2–7, 11–12, 60; as coercive control, 41–42; evaluating, 17–19, 42, 181–82; evidence based, characteristics, 16–17, 146–47; gender-neutral, 164; life-restricting vs. useful, 17, 79, 167; and limitations of NCVS data, 22–23; National Crime Victimization Survey (NCVS), 19–24
Sakaguchi, Kikue, 55–56
Santana, Shannon, 66–67
Sarnquist, Clea, 36
Schaim, Alena, 173–76
Schilling, Dan, 39–41, 170–71
Schleifer, Cyrus, 22
schools: relationship with police, 101, 104, 112; self-defense instruction at, 36; sexual violence at, 28, 30–31, 53, 89, 165; trafficking from, 152
self-confidence: communicating needs and boundaries, 180–81; and intuition, 173–76; second-guessing, 133; and trusting yourself, 72–73; value of, for self-protection, 60
A Self-Defense Study Guide for Trans Women: Because the Stuff that Works for Other People Doesn't Work for Us (TransFighters), 71
self-defense training: communicating needs and boundaries, 180–81; and critical thinking, 177; effectiveness of, 20–21, 35–36, 55, 67–68, 128–31; high-quality, locating, 178–80; misconceptions about, 3; participating in research on, 73; and problem-solving skills, 129; value of, 13, 71–73. *See also* resistance
self-restriction, 79
Senn, Charlene, 35
sex education, 36–37
Sexual Experiences Survey (SES, Koss), 27–28
sexual violence: acquaintance rape, 83; data on, 32, 35; increasing understanding of, 9; media coverage of, 80–82; National Crime Victimization Survey (NCVS), 19–24; non-government data, 32; police handling of, 9, 118–20; preventing, 89; public health data, 26–29. *See also* intimate partner violence; perpetrators
sex work, 52, 70–71, 155
Shapiro, Joe, 33

She Travels Safely, 169–70
"should' statements, 78–79
shouting. *See* verbal resistance
Simpson, Sally, 70
Sinclair Broadcasting, 80–81, 88–89
"smart" women, characteristics, 2
Smith, Nicole, 41
Snodgrass, Sara, 172
Snopes, 151
social justice activism: and creating your own content, 132; linking with personal safety, 16; related to trafficking, 158–59; safety advice that perpetuates stereotypes, 11–12, 144; and understanding trafficking, 154, 157; working for structural change, 8, 16–17
Soriano, Jen, 51–52
stairwells, warnings about, 163–65
Staton, Monte, 23
Stefanik, Elise, 114
Stein, Morris, 45–47
Stein, Stephen K., 57
stimming behavior, 91–92, 103
stranger danger messages: applying critical thinking to, 10, 88; educating people about limitations of, 144; focusing on, limitations of, 141–42; myths about, 77–78; origins and impacts, 138–40; and underreporting of resistance by assault victims, 85–86
Student of Concern policies, 95–96, 103–4
Sun Lakes Sheriff's Department (Arizona), 134

Tark, Jongyeon, 66
Taylor, Lauren R., 13, 179
Telsey, Nadia, 13
Thao, Sheng, 108
"Through a Rapist's Eyes: Pls Take Time to Read This, It May Save a life, it may save your life," 126, 132
TikTok, safety advice on, 47, 126–27, 133–34, 150, 154, 157–58
Tocci, Caroline, 5
Torok, Tashmica, 142
trafficking: as a complex system, 154; education about, 156–57; labor vs. sex, 153–54; role of helplines, 156–57; societal inequities and, 71, 151–54, 157–59; stopping, strategies for, 154–55; unsubstantiated advice about, 149–52
TransFighters, 71
transgender people, 32–34, 70–71
trauma experiences: enduring impacts, 50–52; finding a therapist, 60–61; and hypervigilance, 41–42, 174
Trump, Donald, Trump administration, 29, 105
Turnbull, Oliver, 173

Ullman, Sarah, 64–66, 68
Uniform Crime Report (UCR), 24
United States Census Bureau. *See* National Crime Victimization Survey (NCVS)
Urban Indian Health Institute, 34
U.S. Trans Survey, 33–34

values, personal, and risk tolerance, 178
vans, parking near, myths about in parking lots, 133–34
verbal resistance, 63–65, 69, 129–30, 133, 181
victim blaming: erroneous assumptions about resistance, 4; and male hypervigilance, 41; in media coverage, 82–85; in personal safety directives, 171–72; by police, 87

victim resistance: Bart and O'Brien's study, 65–66; categories of, 65–66; criminalization for, 70–71; studies of effectiveness of, 64, 67–70, 77; study limitations, 70; and time sequence of injury and assault, 65–66; as useless, myths about, 63–64
"victim walk" studies, 8, 45–50, 53–58, 62, 146
violence, gender-based: common myths about, 2–7; complex causes for, 8; dearth of research on, 19; and earlier trauma experience, 50; erroneous assumptions about how to respond to, 2–3; as systemic and political injustice, 177; targeted communities, lack of data about, 21–22
voice, using. *See* verbal resistance

Waechter, Randall, 19
walking style. *See* "victim walk" studies
Walsh, Adam, 138
Walsh, John, 137–39
Washington Post, The Counted database, 32
Webb, Jack, 115
Wheeler, Sarah, 49–50
Wiley-Mydske, Lei, 97–99
windows, myths about, 145–46
Wolf, Dick, 115–16
women. *See* victim blaming
Women Against Crime, 134, 149
Wong, Jennifer, 66
Worthen, Meredith, 22

yelling/shouting, 65, 129–30, 133. *See also* verbal resistance
Youth Risk Behavior Survey (YRBS), 22, 28, 30–31

ABOUT THE AUTHOR

Meg Stone is the executive director of IMPACT Boston, an abuse prevention and empowerment self-defense organization. Her first book, *The Cost of Fear*, addressed gender-based violence and personal safety. She is a recipient of the Visionary Voice Award from the National Sexual Violence Resource Center, which was presented to her by Ayanna Pressley. A nationally recognized leader in the abuse prevention field, Meg was chosen by the US Centers for Disease Control and Prevention as an expert panelist aiding in the development of their standards for preventing sexual abuse in youth-serving organizations. She has also served on the Curriculum Advisory Committee for the US Center for SafeSport, which oversees abuse prevention efforts in US Olympic and Paralympic Sports.

Meg has been an invited speaker at several conferences, including the National Sexual Assault Conference and the Massachusetts Conference for Women. Since 2017, Meg has collaborated with a group of Indigenous women leaders to create a culturally relevant IMPACT program for the Turtle Mountain Chippewa Reservation in North Dakota. It is the first and only Indigenous-led IMPACT program, and Meg raised over $1 million in grant funding to support their work.

Meg's writing has been published in the *Washington Post*, *Newsweek*, *Huffington Post*, the *Boston Globe*, *Dame*, *Ms.*, and several academic and advocacy publications. She is routinely quoted as an expert in publications like *BuzzFeed*, *Shape*, the *Washington Post*, and *Huffington Post*, and she has been interviewed on *PBS News Hour*, C-SPAN, NPR, ABC, and NBC News.